# From Scripture to Life

# CHIARA LUBICH

# From Scripture to Life

New City Press

Published in the United States by New City Press
206 Skillman Avenue, Brooklyn, New York 11211
©1991 New City Press, New York

Translated by Jerry Hearne from the original Italian edition
*Parola che si fa Vita*
©1989 Città Nuova Editrice, Rome, Italy

Cover design by Nick Cianfarani

Library of Congress Cataloging-in-Publication Data:

Lubich Chiara, 1920-
    [Parola che si fa vita. English]
    From scripture to life / Chiara Lubich.
    Translation of: Parola che si fa vita.
    ISBN 0-911782-83-4 : $6.95
    1. Bible. N.T.--Meditations.    2. Christian life--Catholic
  authors.  I. Title.
BS2341.3.L7613   1991
248.4'82—dc20                                                              90-25007

Scriptural quotations are from *The New American Bible*
©1970 Confraternity of Christian Doctrine

Printed in the United States of America

## *Table of Contents*

    Foreword . . . . . . . . . . . . . . . . . . . . . . 7

1. **Put On the Lord Jesus Christ** . . . . . . . . . . . . 10
   *"Put on the Lord Jesus Christ and make no provision for the desires of the flesh"* (Rom 13:14).
       On my way to get the paper . . . . . . . . . . . 13
       A turn around . . . . . . . . . . . . . . . . . . 16

2. **Conversion!** . . . . . . . . . . . . . . . . . . . . . . 18
   *"Give some evidence that you mean to reform"* (Mt 3:8).
       God has won back my heart . . . . . . . . . . 21

3. **The Crucified and Risen Lord** . . . . . . . . . . . . 27
   *"And when I am lifted up from the earth, I shall draw all men to myself"* (Jn 12:32).
       Everyday circumstances, extraordinary results . . . 30

4. **An Offering Well Received** . . . . . . . . . . . . . 33
   *"If you bring your gift to the altar and there recall that your brother has anything against you, leave your gift at the altar, go first to be reconciled with your brother, and then come and offer your gift"* (Mt 5:23).
       A true friend . . . . . . . . . . . . . . . . . . . 36

5. **The Father's Plan** . . . . . . . . . . . . . . . . . . . 38
   *"My food is to do the will of the one who sent me, and to complete his work"* (Jn 4:34).
       Choosing a home . . . . . . . . . . . . . . . . . 41
       Tony and the five dollars shock . . . . . . . . . 43

6. **The New Passover** . . . . . . . . . . . . . . . . . . 48
   *"Get rid of the old yeast to make of yourselves fresh dough, unleavened loaves, as it were; Christ our Passover has been sacrificed"* (1 Cor 5:7).
       I started to live again . . . . . . . . . . . . . . 51

7. **The Greatest Work** . . . . . . . . . . . . . . . . . 57
   *"I solemnly assure you, the man who has faith in me will do the works I do, and greater far than these. Why? Because I go to the Father"* (Jn 14:12).
       A treatment of mutual love . . . . . . . . . . . 60

8. **Believing in Mercy** . . . . . . . . . . . . . . . . . 64
   *"God did not send the Son into the world to condemn the world, but that the world might be saved through him"* (Jn 3:17).
       Anthony's story . . . . . . . . . . . . . . . . . . 68

9. **Before the Eyes of Those Around Us** . . . . . . . . . 71
   *"Whoever acknowledges me before men I will acknowledge before my Father in heaven. Whoever disowns me before men I will disown before my Father in heaven"* (Mt 10:32-33).
       A difficult witness . . . . . . . . . . . . . . . . 74

10. **A Trap Set by Love** . . . . . . . . . . . . . . . . . 79
    *"We know that God makes all things work together for the good of those who love him"* (Rom 8:28).
        My turn as gift . . . . . . . . . . . . . . . . . . 83
        Our blossomed marriage . . . . . . . . . . . . . 85

11. **What Profit is There . . . ?** . . . . . . . . . . . . . 94
    *"What profit would a man show if he were to gain the whole world and destroy himself in the process?"* (Mt 16:26).
        Out to get that money? . . . . . . . . . . . . . 97
        Success at any cost . . . . . . . . . . . . . . . 99

12. **The Rights of God and Those of Caesar** . . . . . . 103
    *"Then give to Caesar what is Caesar's, but give to God what is God's"* (Mt 22:21).
        A manager in Dallas . . . . . . . . . . . . . . 107
        A new rapport . . . . . . . . . . . . . . . . . 109
        Jury duty . . . . . . . . . . . . . . . . . . . . 111

# *Foreword*

From its earliest beginnings, the Christian community—the Church—was built around the Word of God and the Eucharist.

Countless are those, over the centuries, who have drawn near to the Word. Not only has this given rise to the many spiritualities that have enriched the Church, but to the experiences as well of all those Christians whose lives have mirrored the gospel phrase: "Anyone who hears my words and puts them into practice is like the wise man who built his house on rock" (Mt 7:24).

Likewise, our own world of today presents many distinct examples of people who have placed the Word as the basis for their spiritual lives. An authentic experience of the Spirit bears fruit: "He who lives in me and I in him, will produce abundantly" (Jn 15:5).

The material collected in this book is a small gathering of these abundant fruits. They represent the efforts of various members of the Focolare movement, whose beginning in 1943 was marked by a concrete approach to living the Word of God in everyday circumstances. Chiara Lubich, its foundress, in recounting how her adventure began, stated, "These words [of Jesus] appeared to us as spellbinding; they possessed tremendous majesty; they were words of life to be translated into life."[1]

Later, in 1965, Paul VI had defined the Focolare as being

---

1. Chiara Lubich, *A Call to Love* (New York: New City Press, 1989), 82.

already a "mature tree." To mention even briefly what place the Word has held in the course of its development would be a difficult task in such a short introduction. What can be recalled, however, are two principal steps utilized by Chiara and her first group of companions in establishing a relationship with the Word, whether heard during the liturgy or read for meditation. The first step was "to listen to that voice," meaning to be attentive to God's inspirations. In fact, St. Augustine had written, "Look within yourself, for the Truth lies in the intimate of the human person." The second step was that of living the Word.[1] In practice, this meant choosing a phrase of the gospel — a different one each month, for years and decades — to use for reference as a guide toward "reevangelizing" one's own life by applying it to the infinite events of daily life. The result was that over time the gospel as a way of life took its roots, affecting the entire person and had begun to reshape a vast array of societal relationships. A new logic had come into play. Experiences of living the Word of Life[2] were and continue to be reciprocally shared[3] so that its fruits can become common sources of encouragement and light. On such a solid basis of mutual love, the understanding of the scriptures thus creates and gives depth to the Christian community.

The following pages contain commentaries that Chiara Lubich has written on twelve different Words of Life, which the Focolare has put into practice. Each of these

---

1. *Ibid.*, 85.
2. The term "Word of Life" is used among members of the Focolare to refer to that particular phrase of scripture selected month by month for reflection, which is accompanied by a commentary written by its foundress Chiara Lubich, as mentioned. The expression is taken from St. Paul's letter to the Philippians, ". . . you shine like stars in the sky while holding fast to the word of life" (Phil 2:16).
3. St. Teresa of Avila writes: "I don't know why it is not permitted that a person beginning truly to love and to serve God talk with some others about his joys and trials which . . . will benefit himself and those who hear him, and he will come away instructed" (*The Book of Her Life*, ch. 7).

Words of Life is accompanied by lived applications of its teaching. The experiences have been left in the style and form of those who communicated them. Selected from various cultural expressions, they were intended, above all, to be simple gifts to the listener and to the reader. They trace, each in its own way, a passage leading from a personal moment of darkness and confusion to one of light and clarity of purpose.

*The Editor*

# 1.
# *Put On the Lord Jesus Christ*

*"Put on the Lord Jesus Christ and make no provision for the desires of the flesh"* (Rom 13:14).

Whose words are these and to whom were they addressed? The apostle Paul wrote them to the Romans in the conclusion of his exhortation. Applying the image of night and day to the sphere of Christian life, he affirms that the present time is like the night that is already advanced, while the day, that of eternal salvation, is very near.

Therefore, now is the hour to rise up and to cast away the works of darkness; that is, sin, and to put on the armor of light: goodness.

For Paul "putting on what is good," "doing good" is synonymous with "putting on the Lord Jesus Christ," which means his way of being.

Just as when night is over and upon rising in the morning we must put on clothing suitable for the daytime and its activities, so must we, at daybreak, "put on" Christ.

*"Put on the Lord Jesus Christ and make no provision for the desires of the flesh."*

"Put on the Lord Jesus Christ . . ."

Who makes it possible for us to do so?

Baptism has clothed us with Christ and has transformed us into him (cf. Gal 3:27). The expression "to put on" perhaps also refers to the custom at baptism of dressing in new clothing, symbolizing the "new life" the Christian receives, clothing which must be worn well all the way to the end.

For Paul, however, "to put on Christ" means much more: in baptism we have certainly put on the person of Christ (as we join ourselves to him who has died and risen, we die with him and rise with him, meaning we die to sin and are made participants in the new and authentic life of he who is risen), but we can lose this life through sin.

For this reason we must remain faithful to what we have become through baptism and live decisively according to the criteria of the new existence in which we have been placed. Therefore, it is all the more necessary that this new life, as all of life, grow within us to the point of reaching full similarity to Christ.

*"Put on the Lord Jesus Christ and make no provision for the desires of the flesh."*

". . . and make no provision for the desires of the flesh."

To put on Christ demands first of all that we not follow what is in opposition to the Spirit of Christ; that is, the flesh (understood here in its pejorative sense) and its tendencies.

Prior to this statement, Paul lists various disorders of a life lived according to the flesh: excesses in eating and drinking, impurity and lewdness, fights and jealousies, all of which are manifestations of egoism, since one who lives according to the flesh thinks only of oneself, of one's own comfort and satisfaction.

The Christian must abandon all of this and conduct a life in conformity with that of Christ, according to his Spirit, the fruit of which, instead, is love, the gift of oneself, and the continuous service of God and neighbor.

*"Put on the Lord Jesus Christ and make no provision for the desires of the flesh."*

How can we put this Word of Life into practice?
How can we put on Christ?

We have to make our choice courageously, and renew it often, each time as if it were the first.

We must live as Christ, meaning: to love!

These words of Paul, therefore, can be decisive for our lives, as they were for St. Augustine. When reading them, he felt invaded by "a light, almost a certainty," that dissipated his remaining doubts and hesitations to radically change his life, and set him on the course of sanctity (cf. *Confessions* 8:12).

If we allow our hearts to be invaded by the love that comes from the Spirit, all disorderly desires will die out in us; there will be no room left for egoism.

We do not have to perform great things. It's enough that what we are already doing be inspired and animated by true love, whose roots are in Christ.

Living in such a way, we will work toward detoxicating our own selves and the society around us of the many poisons of egoism, which divide and destroy; we will work toward building the civilization of love, which unites people to the Father and among themselves. In this love, all will find their life's fulfillment developing in accordance with their most profound dignity.

*Chiara Lubich*

## *On my way to get the paper*

One Saturday in a restaurant, as I was about to go out to get the newspaper, someone called out my name. I looked, and I faintly recognized the person but I could not think of his name. He realized that I was having a problem but only said that we had been together in a half-way house where he was a resident and I was one of the counselors. I told him that I was just going out front to get a paper and I would be right back. When I went outside I remembered who exactly he was and the memories flooded back . . .

It was very hot in Detroit during the summer of 1972. My supervisor asked me to check on one of the residents who had not been seen for several days. I went to his floor and knocked on his door. He opened it a crack. I asked him to come to the day room. I remember how hot that room was. Someone had turned off the air conditioner and it was like an oven. I sat down and waited for Guy to come in. He appeared in the doorway wearing a sweater that was much too long. The sleeves almost reached to the ends of his fingers. He was pale; ash white would be a better description. I asked if everything was all right and he said he didn't feel well. I got up and touched his forehead. He didn't seem to have a fever. I reached down to take his pulse and he pulled his arm away. It didn't connect right away. I told Guy he could go back to his room.

I sat down trying to figure what was wrong with him. In a matter of seconds I knew exactly what it was. One of the other residents was passing by and I asked him if he would ask Guy to come back to the day room. Before he returned I knew that I had to be a new person for him. I had to be empty so he would be free to say what was wrong. I wanted to be love and nothing but love for him so that it could be Jesus' love he experienced. I tried to put myself in that attitude and hoped I would remain in it.

Guy once again appeared in the doorway. I asked him to sit down. He sat as far from me as possible. I gently asked Guy if he would show me his wrists. He just stared at me with an open mouth. He said, "How do you know?"

Like a little child (Guy was seventeen at the time) he pulled back the sleeves. Both wrists had been cut, not once but several times. The thing to do was to get him to a hospital to be sutured. He said that there was blood on the floor of his room and that he wanted to clean it up before going anywhere. I told him to just relax, I would take care of it.

I went to Guy's room with a bucket of water and a sponge. There was blood splattered on the floor. I knelt down to wipe it up. I thought of how abandoned and alone Guy must have felt, and his situation made me think of Jesus crucified and forsaken on the cross. This thought helped me to do this out of love for Jesus living in Guy.

As I was cleaning up, another young resident came by. We had been having some difficulty with him before but surprisingly he said to me, "Whoever stays in this room probably needs you more right now. I'll finish this." I thanked him and asked him for the keys to his car since at that point I had no way of getting Guy to the hospital except by cab. He reached in his pocket and handed me his keys with a smile.

When Guy and I arrived at the emergency room they put us in an area that was only separated by drape partitions. Guy and I could hear the doctor on the other side. From his tone it was easy to tell he was angry. He was being verbally abusive to the person he was working with. From the conversation both Guy and I understood that the person the doctor was with was a suicide attempt as well. A look of terror came over Guy's face. He became frantic. I put my hand on his shoulder and he calmed down.

The doctor pulled back the curtain, looked at Guy and yelled, "Another one!" Then he looked at me. I smiled. He gave his full attention to Guy. He talked gently but matter-of-factly to him. He told me that he had to report this and that Guy would have to see a hospital social worker. I told him that would be no problem and explained where we were from. Since Guy already had a social worker at the half-way house the doctor asked if the social worker could come back with him when he came to have the sutures removed.

Interestingly enough this doctor eventually volunteered his time, two to three hours a week, to take care of the medical needs of our residents.

Now Guy and I sat and talked over breakfast in this restaurant. He told me about all he had done and gone through over the past fourteen years since that time. He then said, "About the suicide attempt?" I nodded my head. "I want you to know that was the first time I felt loved without being judged. Remembering how you cared has carried me through some very difficult times since then. I have often thought if I could love as you loved me, someone else could experience a new meaning to love."

We exchanged telephone numbers. I have since seen some of Guy's paintings. Some of them speak of love.

*J. K.*

## *A turn around*

I'm a medic in the Air Force and I work in the emergency room. One night we got a call that some gentleman was lying on his living room floor unable to move. So we took the necessary information down and went in the ambulance. When we arrived the neighbors were already there. My partner bent down, got his blood pressure, and did what needed to be done.

He asked the man, "What happened? Did you fall and hit the table?" He totally ignored my partner and would not answer. He asked again, "What happened?" There was still no response. I could see my friend's face getting very red.

A word from scripture which had always fascinated me, came to my mind: "He loved his own in this world, and would show his love for them to the end." I knew what I had to do. I tried to calm my friend as he went out to the ambulance to radio the hospital. Then I returned to the man and asked him what happened. At first he didn't say anything but continued calling for his daughter. He then looked up at me and said, "I have to tell you, I had a few beers, and then I took a whole handful of pills."

Immediately I went through the house looking for empty medication bottles. We then transported him to the hospital. By the time we got there, he had passed out. After a while he came to, becoming violent. He was so angry that no one could calm him. We finally had to strap him down and pump his stomach. He continued to verbally abuse us. My co-worker did not want to take any more of this behavior and since he was now all right, they left, leaving me alone with the man. I had the same feelings that they did, but I remembered I wanted to love him until the end, and so I stayed. As I talked, his anger began to subside and finally he told me why he did it. He wanted to commit suicide and have the insurance money go to his children. I said, "Can I tell you what I personally think?" He nodded for me to go ahead. "I think as a father you are more important to your children than any amount of money you could collect." He just looked at me, and didn't say anything.

At this moment the staff sergeant came into the room and ordered him to say what he had taken. He refused and so they started to argue. The staff sergeant turned around and walked out. The doctor decided he needed some psychiatric help and wanted to send him to another Air Force hospital. Before we could do that, we had to give him a shot to calm down. When he heard this he began to get very angry again and refused to take the injection. I looked at him and asked, "Will you take the shot from me?" To everyone's surprise he answered, "You know I like you, I'll let you give me the shot." So I did.

I had already worked my twelve hours, and I was really tired. They needed two people though, one to drive the ambulance and someone else to stay in the back with him. The hospital they were transferring him to, was three hours distance one way. I wanted to go home really badly but again I remembered that I had to love to the end. So I said, "Okay, I'll stay in the back of the ambulance with him." On the way he slept, because of the shot he had received. When we arrived at the hospital, we left him there and returned home.

About two or three weeks later, he came into the emergency room again, this time with his daughter who had hurt herself. He came up to me and said, "You know I want to thank you, because you were the only one I could talk to." He had felt the love I had shown him, trying to recognize Jesus in him. "I've done a complete turn around," he said, "and I really want to thank you for helping me."

*M. T.*

# 2.
# *Conversion!*

*"Give some evidence that you mean to reform"* (Mt 3:8).

John the Baptist, sent by God to prepare the people of Israel for the coming of the Messiah, preached along the banks of the Jordan words of fire that called for urgent conversion.

He also administered baptism which was the sign of this change of conduct with which Israel was to meet the Messiah. Many sought after him in order to hear his words and to submit themselves to his baptism.

Among them were also members of the sects of the Pharisees and the Sadducees. These were people who thought themselves to be right-minded, and who did not feel, therefore, any need for conversion because they saw themselves as belonging to the chosen people and as being perfect observers of the external precepts of the Mosaic Law, while still neglecting, however, to uphold its spirit.

In their presence, the tone of John the Baptist's message became quite severe. "Brood of vipers!" he warned, "Who told you to flee from the wrath to come? Give some evidence that you mean to reform" (Mt 3:7-8).

*"Give some evidence that you mean to reform."*

What do these words mean? Give proof, by way of concrete facts, that you have undergone a true conversion.

The conversion asked for here by John the Baptist and immediately afterwards by Jesus is a complete turn around in our way of living, a true 180 degree turn. It is a question of putting God at the center of our lives, in the place of our egos and of all earthly things; it is to make his word the norm for all of our thoughts and actions.

The great sin that the Pharisees and Sadducees fell into was that of not having given God his rightful place, and thus replacing what he truly desired with their own interpretations. They gave more importance, for example, to the entire outer facade of religion and cult (ceremonial cleansings, sacrificial offerings in the temple, the rigorous observance of resting on the Sabbath, and so on) than to what God wanted, above all love for and service of one's neighbor.

Jesus will underline more clearly still that it is here especially where the will of God lies.

*"Give some evidence that you mean to reform."*

To put God in the first place, to place him at the center of life itself . . .

Unfortunately, our modern times display a tendency to steer away from God, for he is seen as too demanding, as causing too much discomfort. There are many factors that combine to shape an attitude of simply writing him off as a superfluous and useless being. What is at play is a kind of culture that rests on scientific discoveries and would want to convince us that scientific and technological advances will place humanity in an always better position to tackle, on its own power, all its problems and the conquest of the universe as well. Here lies the great sin of the modern era: the claim to be self-sufficient.

Conversion for many people today, therefore, will consist in accepting or coming to accept again the presence of God in the midst of one's own existence, God without whom humanity is unable to discover its true significance.

*"Give some evidence that you mean to reform."*

There is another way to shun away from God, and this is found in those, instead, who already do believe in him. It is the negligence of not learning how or simply not wanting to live out the practical consequences of their faith.

In fact, we Christians, too, can often recognize ourselves in those Pharisees and Sadducees against whom John the Baptist spoke out so vehemently. How often we bear the name Christian more out of certain habits we have inherited, or because we have received some mere trace of religious instruction, than out of our deep conviction and conscious choice of God! Therefore, do we not reduce our Christianity to traditions and other external practices without committing ourselves to following God's commandments, especially those that regard love of neighbor?

How can we see, then, whether God has his rightful place in our lives?

*"Give some evidence that you mean to reform."*

In what way can we put this Word of Life into practice? We must sincerely examine where we stand before Christ.

Some will realize that they must lovingly welcome that Jesus whom they excluded from their lives. Others will feel the urgency to take his teachings more seriously into consideration.

Others still, who are already following this way of life, will renew the choice of him they have made, perhaps through particular resolutions. The important thing is that we all undergo conversion and reconversion.

One thing is certain. Our world that is so full of wounds can be healed only by Jesus. He asks that we, his disciples, allow him to live in us. We have received his life through baptism, but we need to correspond to it in a decisive way; the gospel, with all it demands, cannot be watered down or be lived in half measures.

If we do take this seriously, we will experience its transforming power. What remains for all of us is just one thing: to convert ourselves concretely, with a show of facts.

*Chiara Lubich*

## *God has won back my heart*

As a child, I did not grow up enjoying the intimate and warm atmosphere typical of a normal family.

The rapport between my parents was hardly ever harmonious and there were continual arguments over money. We children acquired warlike temperaments.

When I was ten years old, we moved from Trent, Italy to the Dolomite Mountains. Immersed in such a stupendous natural setting, I spent six wonderful years feeling free. There I truly experienced moments of full happiness.

After we moved back again to Trent, I continued school but had a rough time with my studies. I flunked twice and finally decided to drop out. I bought a guitar on the very same day. Music and singers had become my passion.

Soon afterwards I also left home. Life had become unbearable. I had found another place to live, where I could still contact friends. We would meet at the snack bars, the town plazas; we conversed, we played, sang, and dreamed. A girlfriend's house became our meeting place, both for ourselves and for others. We ate there, slept there; no schedules to keep, no rules. One day, drugs entered into the picture and made its lasting impression. Our group was very tight-knit and the smoke that we lit up took on the sacredness of a rite.

Among these friends was one who played the guitar exceptionally well and who formed a small musical group. I enjoyed playing with him. Since he had spent a few years in India, I also enjoyed absorbing the Indian culture that he seemed to transmit.

Our friend to whom the house belonged grew tired of this hang-out we had formed. She showed us to the door. I came to meet an eighteen-year-old girl named Silvia. She had already left her family a few years prior and was travelling around, unsettled, throughout Italy.

We had a liking for one another, and decided to stay together. We soon sought a civil marriage. The rock group I continued to play with was doing well and was now performing concerts. Unfortunately, this kept me away from home for lengths of time.

Silvia and I were drifting apart. One day I returned home and saw there was something strange about her. She admitted to have grown tired of being alone; I had become foreign to her life. She met up with heroin.

There was a choice I had to make: it was either Silvia or my music. I chose her. But to save her it must have seemed necessary to me to know what it was like for her to be on this monstrous drug. I started on the needle myself.

Events progressed in rapid fashion. I continued to play the guitar, but at a certain point my life had been taken over. I was addicted and my time had to be spent centered around obtaining the drug. I began to deal heroin, uncut. I was sent to prison twice.

The wild race I was caught up in had come to an abrupt stop. The effect the sudden change had on me was tremendous. My biological and mental patterns were altered. I fell into a deep state of depression. Suicide appeared as the only possible and logical solution. While isolated in my cell, I noticed a hole in the wall. I knew there had once been a hook attached there which someone before me had tried to make use of to put an end to his suffering. If it had only still been there!

The pain at times was so great, since my body was trying to adapt to this quick change. I cried out, but was only laughed at in return.

Finally, I began therapy. This helped me regain my strength and my desire to live. I became more aware of the others imprisoned alongside of me. I played the guitar for them as they found ways to drum out the beat. Once in a while, I called upon God. As soon as I left prison, however, I immediately took again to the needle. So, I found myself back in prison, after which Silvia and I decided to hospitalize ourselves in order to get detoxed.

Our relationship was renewed once again. We wanted to live. Looking back, we did everything together. We were on heroin together; we traveled to India; we entered the hospital together. Yet, at a certain point I decided to leave her.

I was overcome by the weariness of longing to know the purpose of life. I needed something that I didn't know how to define. I knew the whereabouts of some friends who were not on drugs. I headed south. My mother proposed that I move in with one of my uncles, near Florence. I knew that this uncle of mine had something to do with a Christian movement and this disturbed me. I didn't want to know anything about Church, the gospel, or Jesus. Years ago I had broken away from the Church, as I was full of disillusions about people who called themselves Christian.

At the end, however, I accepted the invitation and set out for Florence, where I actually found an atmosphere entirely different from what I had expected. My relatives were well aware of my past, but they never brought up the subject. They showed an incredible respect for me and I began to feel that I could make it back to live a normal life. Hope was born again. I had not yet understood the life my relatives were living, but I had realized one thing: I had found something!

I posed question after question. It was my uncle who offered most of the answers. My aunt, in her silent way, made sure I ate well, that I rested, and that I gained back my strength. A role of even greater importance was played by my cousin, who stayed away from the university for two weeks in order to spend all her time with me. She belonged to the youth section of the same Christian movement and had a way of handling herself that I immensely needed. She didn't say much about herself, but she was always ready to answer my questions. It was enough to look at her; she communicated life.

Summer arrived. My aunt and uncle invited me to a convention that would last four days, where the true turning point of my life began.

Around me I discovered people of all walks of life who were equally animated by the same spirit my relatives lived: young people, people not so young, workers, housewives, children, priests, all involved in building a new world whose only law in guiding human relationships was that of mutual love. Through this experience I became always more convinced that it was not a question of a dreamlike utopia; they were, in fact, very serious about what they were doing.

One morning I ran into a couple of youths. I immediately thought, "Here's a chance to open myself to someone." I confided to them: "Even though my past weighs me down and makes me feel as though I were a hundred years old, here I feel like a newly born baby. Look at me; maybe I'm just a pile of garbage; I can't manage to do anything good, but still, I understand that I cannot waste any more time. I want to begin to live as you do."

Discovery after discovery followed: God is love, Jesus, his gospel. Through the Word of Life that was printed each month, I came to live the phrases of the gospel one by one.

One day, after fifteen years of being away from the sacraments, I sensed an overbearing need of a general cleansing, to immerse my entire soul in this love of God that was coming to me so freely. After my confession, I cried with joy, and the priest cried with me saying "Today there is great joy in heaven." And heaven is now inside of me.

Since that moment, it seems to me that heaven has remained with me and that God had decided to take back his place in my heart. Still, I look for him every day. I choose him and desire him as my greatest treasure. After the convention, life went on with its usual problems, but it seemed to me that everything took its proper place and meaning and I continued to discover that each situation, beautiful or not, carried a sign of God's infinite love.

I had left Silvia behind at the hospital. My relationship with her represented the true dark shadow in my life, while at the same time a new life of universal dimension was opening up within me.

But at this point the Word of Life had become a continual help to me: "Give some evidence that you mean to reform." This is what I felt a dire need for and to which I tried to remain faithful. My entire being seemed to cry out to me that all I needed to do was to love, and the rest would follow through on its own. On my part, I could not fall short to what had been given to me.

How could I explain to Silvia, however, what had been happening to me? I tried first to put it into writing. Then I went to see her. I didn't make any reference at all to my personal experience; I was there totally for her. We took a ride in the car and began a conversation that eventually found her in bitter tears and giving me a forceful slap. For the first time I didn't react poorly. I tried to explain: "I don't know what is happening to me, but trust me." She looked at me despisingly and left slamming the door of the car. She felt betrayed.

Everyone must go his or her own way, but I was certain that the solution would come also for her.

I returned to my relatives. In the meantime, although there were ups and downs, my relationship with Christ, nourished by living his words, was maturing.

So as to learn how to carry this relationship through everyday life in a deeper and more concrete way, I arranged with my relatives to spend a certain period of time at Loppiano.[1] There I worked alongside the others and met various families who lived this spirit with such decision and conviction that they draw others into doing the same. Every so often I wrote to Silvia and we eventually made an appointment to see each other. She still had a jail sentence to complete. Upon leaving, she was disposed to meeting the friends that helped me.

So, later on, for ten days we were guests of a family of the Focolare.

During that short stay, Silvia opened up. Underneath all the gloom, we discovered a Silvia that was pure and transparent and we became very hopeful for her.

In an atmosphere of serenity, she explained to us that she had yet another jail sentence to complete, and that sooner or later she must take care of that one, too. In the meantime, we began to pick up our life together.

As for myself, the adventure of living the gospel continues. Even though I understand that I cannot speak to Silvia about God, I try above all to put into practice with her the concreteness of Christian love. With the help of the families of the Focolare, I found a job and furnished the house. After about a year, Silvia let me know of her desire that our marriage be celebrated in the Church. I felt that this was the effect of the selfless love that surrounded her.

Shortly afterwards, she wanted to reestablish her relationship with her family, especially her father. The day arrived when the police came to escort her to complete her jail sentence. She calmly prepared her luggage. We drove first to the lawyer and then to the jail. There she would hand herself in with the certainty that in that city she would not be alone, for she could now count on our new mutual friends.

In fact, that is where she is now. Through the help of the same

---

1. Loppiano is a well-known locality in Italy, near Florence, the "little city" of the Focolare movement, whose only law is the mutual love that Jesus defines as his "commandment."

family, it was arranged that she could leave prison during the day in order to assist a family in taking care of a handicapped child.

From prison, Silvia writes her new friends and among other things states:

"I must learn how to pronounce a simple 'thank you' but it is not so easy for me. At one time, the little I had, I had to sweat for, and I was convinced that it was due to me. Now, I see things differently! Now, I am certain that whatever I have is superfluous, because I have received what girls like myself have rarely received. When I was out of prison last time, I could not do other than let myself be guided by such wonderful people.

"You came to me . . . as I was closed within my shell. Suddenly I discovered myself; I can finally begin to accept myself for who I am! I can love. If I look around me, I can't help but feel privileged. I know there is someone I must particularly thank, someone much higher than us, but at least for now I am able to say thanks to all of you! Who knows, perhaps one day I will arrive up there; for now I limit myself to say that I don't find any more words to say . . . but I'm very happy!"

*M. and A. B.*
*(Italy)*

# 3.
# The Crucified and Risen Lord

*"And when I am lifted up from the earth, I shall draw all men to myself"* (Jn 12:32).

These words of Jesus are stupendous. Here lies the key to Christianity. This passage was proposed to all Christians for meditation during the week of prayer for Christian unity.

Passover was near, and in the crowd of pilgrims that was gathered in Jerusalem, there were some Greeks. They asked "to see Jesus." When the disciples brought them over to him, Jesus immediately spoke to them of his imminent death. He added that his death, rather than disperse his disciples, as could have happened, would draw "all" to himself: not only his own, but anyone, Jew or Greek, who would believe in him—all people, without distinction of race, social condition, or sex (cf. Gal 3:28).

In fact, Jesus' work of salvation is universal and the presence of the Greeks is a sign of this universality. Their desire to see Jesus is an indication that "the hour has come" for him "to be lifted up."

*"And when I am lifted up from the earth, I shall draw all mèn to myself."*

What does it mean "when I am lifted up from the earth"?

For John the Evangelist, this expression means at once "to be lifted up on the cross" and "to be glorified." In fact, John sees in the passion and death of Christ the great demonstration of God's love for humanity. This love is so powerful that it merits the resurrection and causes the attraction of everyone to him. The unity of the new people of God will be built around Christ who is lifted up.

The cross, therefore, is no longer a sign of malediction and death. Jesus has transformed it into a means of victory over sin, which is death in its true form.

The cross can no longer be separated from glory; the crucified Christ cannot be separated from the risen Christ. They are two aspects of the same mystery of God who is love.

Divine love is an attracting force. The crucified-risen Lord sparks in the human heart a deep and personal attraction that takes on two particular forms: Jesus calls his own to share in his glory, and at the same time he brings them to love everyone as he did, to the point of giving their lives.

*"And when I am lifted up from the earth, I shall draw all men to myself."*

How can we live this Word of Life? How can we respond to such great a love?

Let us try to accept into our hearts and to put into practice this precious teaching of the crucified-risen Lord. It will shed light also on the role that suffering plays in our lives and on its extraordinary fruitfulness.

Day after day, as we are struck by small or great sufferings, which may surface as a doubt, a failure, a misunderstanding, a tense relationship, a problem at work, a sickness, even a disgrace of some sort or a situation of serious concern, let's make the effort to accept them and to offer them to Jesus as an expression of our love.

Let us join our little drop to the sea of his passion so that it can work for the good of many, of those dearest to us, or for the Church: let us unite it to his passion for peace among all peoples, and in this month particularly, for the unity of Christians.

Once we have made our offering, let's try not to think about it anymore, but accomplish in that moment what God wants from us. Whether we be with our family, at the warehouse, in the office, at school, let us above all else try to love others, to love those who are around us.

If we do so, we will be able to experience something unusual and unexpected: our souls will be invaded with peace, love, light, and even pure joy. We will find a new strength within us. We will see how, by embracing our daily crosses and by uniting ourselves through them to Jesus crucified and forsaken, we can participate in his risen life already here on earth.

Enriched with this experience, we will more effectively be able to help our brothers and sisters find the beatitude that lies deep within their tears, and transform into serenity that which afflicts them. In this way we will become channels of joy for many people, channels of happiness, of that happiness to which every human heart aspires.

*Chiara Lubich*

## *Everyday circumstances, extraordinary results*

I am a university student and this past semester I took an architecture design class along with my usual schedule of classes. The first day of class already gave me a good idea how this particular class would be. After I saw the syllabus of work to be done and the list of necessary materials I thought seriously about dropping such an outrageous class. In fact, after that first day half of the students dropped it. I decided to stay since at that time I was still trying to choose my field of study and I thought this course would be a good introduction to architecture.

As the semester went along the teacher expected more and more from us to the point that I felt I was working day and night only for this class. The heavy workload made many of the students very resentful and, at times, discouraged. Our teacher was not a very popular person and the students avoided her as much as possible.

Towards the end of the semester all the students were both frustrated and tired and many stopped coming to classes altogether except on days when they had to hand in an assignment. The final blow came when we were assigned a major project, a project that required more materials, work and time than any of the previous ones. We were told that on a certain day we were to bring all our work to class so that she could see the progress we were making. Many of the students decided that they would just skip that class and do their work at home. When the day arrived I was also strongly tempted to do the same but I thought of our teacher. Certainly she must have been aware of all the bad feelings in the class and the resentment towards her. I decided that out of love for her I would take everything and go to the class even if no one else bothered to come.

In fact that day in class we were only three. When the teacher arrived she looked around but said nothing. She came over to me and asked to see my work. As I showed her my project she began to verbally tear it apart and when she had commented on everything I had done she started to criticize me, saying that I should never have even been in the class because she had no time to waste teaching such basic things and this went on for at least half an hour. When she finished I felt so bad that I took a break and left the room.

I walked around the campus trying to figure out what had happened. I had gone to the class out of love for her and look what had happened. It just didn't make sense. Then I remembered Jesus on the cross when he felt forsaken by his Father; even in that moment he had continued to love. I realized then that I had to go back to the class and try to love my teacher even in this absurd situation.

When I got there, I went to her and asked what suggestions she might have for my project. We went over the project from start to finish, making all the plans for its completion and afterwards she seemed to be very happy.

After this experience I tried even harder to do all my work out of love for her. During the last week of school I saw her walking towards the classroom alone. I said hello and started to walk beside her. For the first time she began to talk to me telling me about her husband and her family and many other things. From that moment a new relationship was established between us that went beyond that of teacher-student. I felt she thought of me as a friend.

Besides going to school I also have been working part time for the past two years for a printing company. In the time that I have been there I have worked in just about every area of the company, from driving the delivery truck to doing the bookkeeping, and I have a pretty good idea about the way things work and what needs to be done.

One day we had a couple of big printing jobs and I worked most of the day folding one of the orders while another man was working at trimming and packaging the other job. In the afternoon he left for some reason and I went ahead with the job I had been doing. As soon as I finished I went to the front office and saw my boss. He asked me how the other job was going and I told him that right now no one was working at it. He didn't seem to be too happy about that and I could see that he was really under a lot of pressure to finish that particular job. I went back to work on another order that had come in and soon my boss walked by asking how the other job was going. When he saw that still no one was working on it he turned and started yelling at me, asking why I wasn't doing my job! He told me to immediately get to work on the other job and he stormed off.

At first I was shocked. In the two years that I had been there he had never criticized me for my work and he had never raised his voice at me. I became furious myself, indignant that he would have said such things to me. I was about to go after him into his office and start yelling when I remembered that also Jesus on the cross had suffered a terrible injustice and that what I felt was just a small fraction of his tremendous suffering. In trying to unite my suffering to his I felt a great peace, and I knew then that the only solution was to love even in this circumstance.

I decided that I would finish the entire job out of love for my boss especially since I knew that it was the pressure to get it finished that was making him so tense and nervous.

After that decision the job I was doing was not really work, it was joy. I finished in no time, and when I later saw my boss I told him not to worry, that it was all taken care of. When I said that, his face lit up. "Really?" he said. "Thanks, I knew I could count on you."

After I had been working for this printing company for a while they hired a young girl who had just graduated from high school. She spoke very little and hardly ever smiled.

One day we had a big book that needed to be put together and stapled so I was working that day in the bindery. There was a lot of work to do so the boss asked Janet to help me. It was not a very exciting job — it consisted of walking back and forth picking the pages from the table and putting them together.

After we had been working for awhile in silence we started to talk a little. I asked her about her family and she slowly started to tell me an almost unbelievable story. When she was only eight, her older brother had been killed and her life had consisted of a number of serious tragedies involving other family members.

The more she talked, the more I realized the pain and sufferings she had gone through. I knew it was not my place to try and give her answers, but since she felt confident enough to share all these things with me, I could take these sufferings upon myself and bear them as if they were mine.

Before leaving that day she told me how happy she was to know someone who could really understand her sufferings.

*P. M.*

# 4.
# An Offering Well Received

*"If you bring your gift to the altar and there recall that your brother has anything against you, leave your gift at the altar, go first to be reconciled with your brother, and then come and offer your gift"* (Mt 5:23).

This is one of those teachings of Jesus that, if understood well, can incite a true revolution within us, and if it were lived by everyone in the world, peace would be assured for all time.

Jesus imagines that an Israelite is on his way to the temple to offer his sacrifice to God. Today, we can think of someone who is on the way to church in order to attend Mass.

In the time of Jesus, the sacrificial offering for an Israelite — as it would be today for a Christian who attends Mass — is representative of the most important moment, the highest form of one's relationship with God. Well then — Jesus says, speaking in paradoxical terms in order to underline the importance God gives to full accord between brothers and sisters — if, as you are about to offer your sacrifice, you recall that there is some disharmony between yourself and your neighbor, put aside your sacrifice and go first to be reconciled with your neighbor.

The sacrificial offering in fact — for we Christians it would be our participation at Mass — would run the risk of losing its meaning if we were in disaccord with our brothers and sisters. The principal sacrifice that God expects of us is that we do our best to be in harmony with everyone.

*"If you bring your gift to the altar and there recall that your brother has anything against you, leave your gift at the altar, go first to be reconciled with your brother, and then come and offer your gift."*

At first sight, this particular exhortation may make it appear that in Jesus' thought there isn't anything substantially new in respect to the Old Testament. In fact, the prophets had already anticipated this concept as they spoke of how God prefers, over holocausts, love of neighbor, mercy, and compassion toward the weak (cf. Hos 6:6). When sacrifices are offered by persons who oppress the poor, he considers them as loathsome (cf. Is 1:10-20). Rather than being acts of praise, they become insults to God.

But its novelty does exist and it lies here: Jesus affirms that we must always be the ones who take the initiative to assure the harmony of our relationships, to safeguard fraternal charity. He reveals the commandment of love for neighbor at its deepest roots. In fact, he does not say: if you recall having offended your brother, but: if you recall that your brother has anything against you. For Jesus, to remain indifferent in the face of any disharmony in our relationships, even though we ourselves are not the cause of that disharmony, and the others are, is already reason for not being well received by God, for being rejected by him.

Jesus, therefore, wants to put us on guard not only against the wildest outrages of hatred, but also against any kind of expression or attitude that in some way may show a lack of consideration and love toward our neighbors.

*"If you bring your gift to the altar and there recall that your brother has anything against you, leave your gift at*

*the altar, go first to be reconciled with your brother, and then come and offer your gift."*

How can we put these words into practice?

We must try to avoid being superficial in our relationships with others, and to make use of the most hidden recesses of our hearts. In this way we will also overcome any kind of indifference, lack of goodness, or any air of superiority or neglect toward anyone.

Normally, we try to make up for an act of rudeness, or outbreak of impatience by asking pardon or by extending a gesture of friendship. If, at times, this is not possible, what counts is our complete inner change of attitude. An attitude of instinctive rejection of our neighbor must be replaced by one of complete openness, of total acceptance of the other, of boundless mercy, forgiveness, sharing, and concern for the other's needs.

If we act in this way, we can offer to God any kind of gift we wish, and he will accept it and keep it in mind. Our relationship with him will be deepened and we will reach that union with him which will be our true happiness in the present day and in the future.

*Chiara Lubich*

## *A true friend*

Because of my credentials I was placed in a position of authority over other people who worked on my shift. Several of these people had worked at the corporation for up to ten years. Some of them resented my being placed in a position of authority over them. What they resented even more was that I held them to corporation rules and policies. Another underlying problem was that I was of a different race than the rest of the staff and there were walls of mistrust.

Tension on the job built up between myself and one other worker. At one point he exploded, calling me several names in front of ten of our clients. This gesture undermined my authority, because our clients liked this worker very much. He also said that he would have to request a transfer to another facility that the corporation owned which was half again as far from his home than our facility. He said he would have to do this to avoid becoming violent with me. He didn't want to beat me up and cause his brother, the executive director, to lose a good employee, he added. He saw me as a good worker, but one that he couldn't get along with.

He went ahead and requested the transfer, and for six months, drove an hour more each day just so that he would not have to work with me as his superior. One day while at work at the other facility he suffered a mild heart attack. This now made it impossible for him to safely make the trip to and from the facility so far from his home. Therefore he came back to our facility.

Luckily, I had learned many things about authentic Christian living and especially how to build unity in the meantime. Before arriving at work I would pause momentarily and tell God that I really wanted this worker, who had become an "enemy," to feel only love from me. At work I would always say hello to him as I would to a true friend. But that wasn't enough. I had learned that Christians have to love concretely. Since he was recovering from a heart attack, I decided that I could help him gradually recover his strength by inviting him to a health club with me. He had been an excellent football player in his younger years and suffered greatly now from being weak and having little physical endurance.

He accepted and I went to his home early every other day, and took him to my health club. He and I went through months of serious workouts and I gradually coached him back to health. During each workout we talked and it became as much an enjoyable social event as it was a physical one.

During this time my supervisor resigned. I really wanted the job, because besides the experience and increased pay, it would allow me to work better hours. I had been working every weekend for eighteen months, and I was tired of being away from my wife every weekend. To my surprise, this gentleman wrote a letter to his brother, the executive director, recommending that I be given the job. I could hardly believe it! I got the promotion.

When my baby was baptized, this man called and said he wanted to prepare all the food for the christening party, free of charge. He said he wanted to do it because I had helped him recover his strength after his heart attack. The meal was a wonderful full-course dinner, perfectly prepared for over twenty people.

*M. M.*

# 5.
# *The Father's Plan*

*"My food is to do the will of the one who sent me, and to complete his work"* (Jn 4:34).

This is a marvelous affirmation of Jesus which every Christian can, in a certain way, repeat of oneself, and if lived out is capable of leading us very far on life's holy journey.

Jesus, seated by the well of Jacob, in Samaria, is nearing the close of his conversation with the Samaritan woman. The disciples, having returned from the nearby town where they went to gather provisions, were astonished to see the master speaking with a woman. No one asked him why he was doing so, and when the woman left, they invited him to eat. Jesus had an intuition of what was on their minds and he explained to them what moved him to act, saying, "There is a food I must eat that you do not know about."

The disciples did not understand: they were thinking of a material food, and they asked each other whether, while they were away, someone had brought the master some food. Jesus very openly told them:

*"My food is to do the will of the one who sent me, and to complete his work."*

We need to have food every day in order to sustain our

lives. Jesus does not deny this. And here he speaks precisely of food, of its natural necessity, but he does this to give affirmation to life and the need of another kind of food, a very important food, of which he cannot do without.

*"My food is to do the will of the one who sent me, and to complete his work."*

Jesus came down from heaven in order to do the will of the one who sent him and to complete his work. He does not have any thoughts or plans but those of his Father's; the words he speaks and the works he accomplishes are those of the Father; he does not do his own will, but the will of the one who sent him. This is the life of Jesus. Living in this way satisfies his hunger. This is how he nourishes himself.

His life is characterized by his full adherence to the Father's will, all the way to death on the cross, where he will truly bring to completion the work his Father entrusted to him.

*"My food is to do the will of the one who sent me, and to complete his work."*

Jesus considers doing the Father's will his food, because by accomplishing it, "assimilating it," "eating it," identifying himself with it, he receives life.

What is the will of the Father, his work, that Jesus must bring to completion?

It is to bring salvation to humankind, to give to humanity that life that does not die.

Jesus, just moments before, through his love and his words, communicated a seed of this life to the Samaritan woman. In fact, the disciples will soon see this life bud forth and spread out because this Samaritan woman will communicate the richness she discovered and received to other Samaritans: "Come and see someone. . . . Could this not be the Messiah?" (Jn 4:29).

Jesus, as he was speaking to the woman, revealed to her the plan of God the Father: that all people might receive the gift of his life. This is the work that Jesus presses on to complete, so that he can entrust it then to his disciples, to his Church.

*"My food is to do the will of the one who sent me, and to complete his work."*

Can we ourselves live this word so typical of Jesus, so as to be a reflection, in a very particular way, of his being, his mission, and his zeal?

Certainly!

We too will have to live out our true being, that of sons and daughters of the Father through the life that Christ has communicated to us; we will have to nourish our lives on his will.

We can do so by accomplishing moment by moment what he wants from us, by completing it perfectly as though we had nothing else to do. This is what Pope John XXIII proposed for his own life. God, in fact, does not want any more than this.

Let's nourish ourselves then with what God wants from us moment after moment and we will experience that living in this way will satisfy our hunger: it will give us peace, joy, happiness, and a foretaste—it is not an exaggeration to say so—of heavenly bliss.

In doing so, we too, will join Jesus, day by day, in completing the work of the Father, which is our own salvation and that of many others.

*Chiara Lubich*

## *Choosing a home*

*Jim:* About a year ago my company transferred me back to Indianapolis. After renting for about six months, Millie and I decided to buy a house. Since we have been trying to put the gospel into practice with other decisions in our lives, we agreed that we wanted to make this choice of a house in the same way.

Our family situation was that our four daughters were now young adults; the youngest was about to finish college. Our daughters are close in age so we had a period of five years when three of them were in college at the same time. We were beginning to breathe a little easier now because these high-expense years were almost over.

So we set out to find a house that would be a good home for "just the two of us," but also for our family and friends. We saw a great variety of houses: the traditional house and yard, condominiums, and so on. They ranged from modest and simple to the very luxurious. I was very attracted to some of them: to those we could afford, and also to some that we could not.

*Millie:* Some were extravagant. The kind of car you owned seemed to determine your suitability for that neighborhood. We realized also that some complexes did not foster a family atmosphere, or focus on family needs. Their design was for adult living. There were separate swimming pools for adults and children, for example. We knew this could not be our life-style.

After looking for weeks, I began to feel tired and frustrated. I began to want more than we had set out to find. "Don't we deserve this, after years of hard work? Why should we not have more room, a bigger yard?" It all seemed so tempting again. Then we reminded each other of our choice to put God first.

*Jim:* I remember taking a deep breath and asking Millie, "Are we following Jesus?" We talked about the gospel lesson of being a good steward and it reminded us that having only what we needed would be enough for us. Also we remembered that we had wanted our house to be a means to serve others. After all, in the gospel Jesus says, "If anyone would serve me, let him follow me; where I am, there will my servant be."

I felt I was now finally house-shopping for someone else: for Millie, for our daughters and others. Those things that had come to seem so important no longer mattered.

*Millie:* Then we spoke to each of our daughters and let them know where we were with our house selection so that they could tell us what they thought. One by one, they seemed to understand what we were doing and were happy with our choice.

Now that we are settled, and have gone through a couple of holidays with the family, we see that by not having such a big home, with many rooms to escape to, we work together to keep it organized and have more respect for each other's needs.

*Jim:* One experience of this happened at Christmas time. Our three single daughters were planning to come home from Texas, South Carolina, and Purdue University to stay for about a week. Millie and I agreed this would be the test because the girls wouldn't have all the space at their disposal as they did before.

We turned the den into a guest bedroom . . . and we had visions of what would happen with our three daughters cramped in this area for a week. It was a struggle for us because we wanted them to feel welcome, we wanted to provide a peaceful place for them to be. Finally we had the idea of giving our upstairs bedroom and bath to them. It would be much more spacious and "invisible from downstairs." So we moved into the guest bedroom. The girls really enjoyed the "college dorm" atmosphere with each other and we all experienced some "peace on earth" for Christmas.

*Millie:* With the choice of this home we have experienced more financial freedom for ourselves, as well as the freedom to help others. Since we have less to take care of, we have been able to spend more time with friends and family. Also, we realized that we had furniture that we no longer needed in a smaller house. We decided not to save it but to offer it to others. I experienced great joy and found it very freeing. I wondered if this might not be how the early Christians felt.

*Jim:* I am experiencing peacefulness in this house. Perhaps it is because this is where God wants us to be right now. It reminds me of something else Jesus says: "If anyone loves me, he will keep my word, and my father will love him and we will come to him, and make our home with him."

*J. and M. P.*

## *Tony and the five dollars shock*

Tony was slumped over the telephone in the corner of the warehouse, staring glassily into space, breathing heavily. We had found him like this once before. It took us a long time to sober him up.

The next day, walking along the street with a friend, I saw Tony again. This time he was slumped against a wall, on the opposite side of the street. He was begging for change from the passersby. Together my friend and I tried to get him to his feet; it was impossible. We dragged his almost deadweight to the closest hospital.

It seemed impossible that he had gone downhill so completely. I had known him for eighteen years, ever since he had been appointed to our office. Over the years we had noticed an increase in the lack of balance in one who already was far from stable. It was common knowledge that he had been in mental hospitals several times; but even so, no one had really guessed the whole truth, nobody knew what his illness was.

Now, in the street, as I lifted up the full sweaty weight, and recognized the telltale smell of his breath and the glazed daze in his eyes, for the first time I knew with painful certainty what I had only vaguely suspected: Tony's sickness was that insatiable thirst which dominates and never releases those whom it has enslaved, and which more and more was forcing him to drown his defeats in alcohol.

To drag his inert body to the hospital was physically exhausting but what weighed even more heavily on me was the weight of his failure, of his inadequacy in life. As we struggled along I realized with utmost clarity that I was not going to be able to be relieved of his "weight" once I had left Tony in the hospital.

The very next day I went to see the office supervisors about him. Tony was employed in my section and I had to take some steps concerning him. I asked them for some time before they resorted to such drastic measures as dismissal. I took on total responsibility for his case. My next step was to meet his wife.

I sent a message to Tony's wife and the next day, when I

arrived for work at eight o'clock, she was standing by my desk. She was worn out and hollow-eyed with exhaustion. She told me that the day before, she had been to all the main newspaper publishers in the city, asking for help for her family. "In a city of four million people," she told me, "I felt completely alone!"

As she slowly unfolded her story, I stepped, with her, into a nightmare. She had three children, one eight, one six and one four years old. They were living a nightmare relationship with a father who was almost always drunk. The youngest one in particular would run terrified to hide under the bed every time his father came home; he would stay there until Tony left the house.

There it was. Tony drank, and had been drinking—and drinking immoderately—for twenty years. At first he had managed to hide the fact, but now he could no longer control himself.

His wife went on to tell me about their life together; their friends and even their family had practically deserted them. To provide some sort of stability for the family, she had taken a job as a nurse in a nearby hospital, working nights so as to be with the children during the day.

There was nothing I could say. It did not seem right to comment with sterile words of conventional encouragement on all that poured out from her. All I could say to her was that among the four million people in the city she now had at least one friend, and she must never feel alone again.

In the days that followed I got hold of her husband's medical records, and took them to a medical friend of mine. Immediately he faced me with the fact that Tony's alcoholism was so far advanced that there was little to no chance of his ever recovering. However, I discovered that in the city there was a branch of Alcoholics Anonymous (A.A.), a group of people who are ex-alcoholics and who dedicate their lives to the rehabilitation of those still addicted. I took my colleague's case to them. I went straight to their headquarters. What struck me most about these people was their availability, their immediate willingness to put aside everything in their daily life in order to help another alcoholic be rid of this oppressive bondage.

Tony was due to come out of the hospital any time, and I told the organization that I wanted their help in keeping him in his job. The president of the association promised to help me, and advised me to bring Tony by as soon as possible.

It was five o'clock in the evening when I finally was able to call Tony's home and talk to his wife about this new development. I asked her how best to present it to her husband. She was utterly pessimistic. She already knew about A.A. Tony had always refused to have anything to do with them or their meetings. I asked her to try once more; I suggested that she tell him a friend was coming to take him to meet some people who would help him.

A few days later I went to the hospital to meet him when he was discharged. He was dumbfounded when he saw me. "What are you doing here?" he asked. "Why are you going through all this trouble for me?" I told him right away that I was "the friend" who was to help him, and taking advantage of his surprise, I got him into the car and drove straight to the headquarters of A.A.

The group which Tony was in met three times a week. During these meetings I always sat next to him in absolute silence. I felt it could be important for him to have a friend next to him, ready to receive the first flicker of his intention to recover, and to encourage him on. In spite of all this, he began drinking again. Sometimes, with his wife, I carried him bodily from the car into the meeting room, but throughout the sessions he would sit and stare at me with a faraway, vacant expression in his eyes.

We carried on like this for about four long months. Life had become a battleground. I would get home at eleven o'clock or midnight, utterly exhausted, having used up every last ounce of energy encouraging Tony's wife—who returning home from the sessions could no longer restrain her tears nor maintain her hope—to go on one more day . . . and then another . . . and then another: all seemingly the same, an ever-increasing total of defeats and disappointments.

Inside myself I knew that I could not give up. I had chosen to help Tony, and I was ready to go on, seated silently next to him, for who knows how many more meetings. One evening as I was going home, a phrase from the gospel came to my mind; it seemed to mirror exactly the situation I found myself in: "He had loved his own in the world, and would show his love for them *to the end*" (Jn 13:1). This, it seemed to me, had to be the measure. We had to love Tony to the end. To the end of his illness? I didn't know. It just had to be . . . to the end.

The very next day the president of Alcoholics Anonymous took me to one side and admitted that Tony was one of their most difficult cases. In fact, he was almost irrecoverable. There was only one more thing to try, he said, and that was shock. As his friend, I had to talk to him seriously—even severely—and shock him into facing reality.

Before speaking to Tony, I went to pray in the silence of a church. I asked myself over and over again whether I really loved him to the point of giving my life for him. Only on this condition could I speak to him so harshly.

Tony was not expecting me that day. He was surprised and then stunned by our conversation. I had never spoken to him like that before. I told him that he was to have his last chance: that his wife (and this was true), having given up all hope of his recovery, was on the point of abandoning him.

As his superior in the firm I forbade him to ask for any more loans from the company, and I added that I too had come to the end of my rope. I said that since he had decided to continue forever on this road, I would give him five dollars per day so that he would have the means of dying as quickly as possible, thereby freeing his wife and children of his presence. With that I went away, leaving the first five dollars crumpled in his hand.

I waited two hours in the most acute anxiety ever, waiting to see his reaction. At last he came to my office, trembling from head to foot, his eyes full of tears. He begged me not to abandon him as I was the only person he could count on who really cared for him.

Once again I went with him to the meetings of the ex-alcoholics, and two evenings later I saw him—after all those months—take the first positive step towards recovery admitting in front of others that he was an alcoholic and sincerely expressing his desperate need to stop drinking.

This was the moment of truth! He had struck the bedrock on which we together could build—a realization on the psychological level no one had even dared to hope for.

For another two weeks Tony continued to drink, but then finally—and painfully, at first—he gave it up and began his new life with no further lapse.

At last, Tony, helped by the methods of his friends in the group put his whole effort into breaking the chains of the past. After twenty years of torment, he was beginning to rebuild relationships, first with his wife, then with other people. This took months, but eventually I watched him take the first steps towards helping other alcoholics inside the group, approaching the newly arrived, especially those who, at that stage, were worse than he.

Then, one day, he asked me to go with him to a nearby town. He said he had a surprise for me. He was going to open there a new branch of Alcoholics Anonymous. It was wonderful! I heard him address with absolute confidence a capacity audience, but that was not the surprise. At last it came. He said — among other things — that once he was free from alcohol, he felt love for his children, and he spoke of the deep affection which now united him to that little one who had previously fled from him in terror.

"It is nothing short of a miracle," Tony's wife said to me. "And I just don't know how to thank you! I've thought about it for a long time. In the end I felt inside myself that there was only one thing that I had to do. I took my three children and we went to church. I, who have not set foot inside a church in years, went with the children to pray for you. But that is not the end. On Sunday, for the first time, Tony came with us to Mass."

R. C.

# 6.
# *The New Passover*

*"Get rid of the old yeast to make of yourselves fresh dough, unleavened loaves, as it were; Christ our Passover has been sacrificed"* (1 Cor 5:7).

The word we now turn to for meditation and which we want to live is one that, if understood well, brings joy and strength to our hearts, for it gives clarity to our lives as Christians. In fact, the followers of Christ are not always fully aware of the divine greatness that is theirs, of their mark of distinction, and their sublime dignity, all due to God's love for them.

The word for this month is one that offers fascination and can give our lives, which may be barely trudging along, a new set of wings. It makes us aware of the immense treasure we already possess, though often unknowingly.

To find a way to communicate this reality, Paul takes his cue from the Passover feasts. The Mosaic Law prescribed that in the Passover celebration only unleavened bread may be used. The house, from the very first day, was made ready top to bottom and any trace of leavened bread was taken away. During Passover, in fact, the Jews recalled and relived their great liberation from slavery in Egypt, and the unleavened bread reminded them how hurriedly they had to leave Egypt that very night. Later on, this bread also came to symbolize purity and integrity.

The apostle Paul sees in this event a figure of the Christian Passover. As the Israelites celebrated their Passover by removing leavened bread from their homes, so the Christians of Corinth, to whom he writes, ought to celebrate the new Passover, their resurrection with Christ which took place in baptism, by eliminating the bread of old from their ways of conduct. The bread of old stood for any seed or remaining trace of their old mentality, any inclination whatsoever to the evil that was a part of their former lives.

This new Passover which Paul referred to, however, was not the one recorded on the calendar, but rather it was the communion lived with the risen Lord who is within us and which can occur on a daily basis. It was, in each moment, the passage from the slavery of sin to new life in Christ: a Passover that would last for a lifetime.

*"Get rid of the old yeast to make of yourselves fresh dough, unleavened loaves, as it were; Christ our Passover has been sacrificed."*

You are "unleavened loaves." If we look carefully, we can see that on the one hand, Paul urges us to throw away the old bread, supposing therefore, that it still exists within us. On the other hand, he tells us that we are already unleavened; that is, without yeast. This can be puzzling, but in reality there is no contradiction. In fact, by the power of our resurrection with Christ and of the life of grace that we have received from him, we can truly say that at this point we are unleavened, meaning we are new creations: our passions have certainly not the power to enslave us and cling onto us to the extent they once had.

It is always true, however, that even after our birth into the new life, the roots of our "old self," our old instincts, still remain. If we are not vigilant, they can sprout up again and lead us to sin. Here we must be watchful and fight hard in order to eradicate them.

In essence, through his warning Paul wants to tell us: be sure that your personal conduct reflects the new reality which you are; be sure that this new life that is already within you blossoms and grows, and that you bring it to its fullness.

*"Get rid of the old yeast to make of yourselves fresh dough, unleavened loaves, as it were; Christ our Passover has been sacrificed."*

How can we live this Word of Life?

We can do so by focusing on three very important elements for our lives as Christians. First of all, we need great faith; that is, the deep-rooted conviction that the grace of Jesus is much stronger then the inclination to sin which we still carry within us.

Secondly, we need great generosity in our commitment to dig out the seeds of sin, the roots of the vices which we still possess.

Finally, we need to animate our generosity with a boundless trust in the mercy of Jesus; that trust which drives us to always begin over again, even after every eventual failure.

In fact, we must not deceive ourselves; it will perhaps be a long way down the road before we take these roots away. Jesus, however, will not judge us on how long it took and on the results of our efforts, but rather on the basis of the readiness, and this presupposes humility and trust, with which we get back on our feet each time we fall. In essence, Jesus will bring ahead the work of our sanctification in the measure in which we learn to believe in his love.

*Chiara Lubich*

## *I started to live again*

*Miguel:* I was always in search of something that would give meaning to my life. At times, invited by friends, I attended prayer meetings. The sense of well-being I experienced from them usually lasted for a very short time, a few minutes, a few days, at best for several months. Despite my efforts and attempts to encounter God, I would still only find an emptiness inside. . . . Invariably, I would go back to being as I was before.

I was a heavy drinker. I really drank a lot. As one thing led to another, I became unfaithful to my wife. My drinking she would forgive, but this, no. Since she first discovered it, my error became a weapon in her hands, which she used both to defend herself and to attack. Practically speaking, we were tearing each other to pieces; the family was breaking down. If we continued to live under the same roof, it was out of love for our children, the only thing that could keep us together. And what about love? My own behavior had nothing to do with love, though maybe it did reveal a certain respect or a sense of responsibility. To reach love I had far to go. While I actually believed I was loving, in essence, there wasn't a drop of love between us; we lived as though we were separated from one another.

I came to meet Father Venanzio. With him I was able to speak about my understanding of the gospel (which I thought I knew very well) . . . and I would always be the one speaking. Father Venanzio always listened. It was a phenomenon that was new to my life: someone was listening to me! We went on like this for a long time. He took me by surprise one day, however, when he invited me to a meeting, which he said gathered together people who took the gospel seriously and through the gospel received the light, joy, and strength to live out their daily lives. "A wonderful life," he added, "you really have to get to know it."

I was never too keen about meetings of this kind. The gospel was something I could handle in theory, but its application to life? I tried to shrug off his invitation by answering, "But, Father, these things are not for me." All the same, due to the great respect I held for him, I found myself in the midst of a couple of hundred people, about to make an experience that I never would have imagined.

Father Venanzio made use of his astuteness: he sent two exceptional young men to ride with me by car, one reason so that they themselves could get to and from the meeting; the second reason, so that I wouldn't cop out. In fact, I had planned to slip away after the first day of the meeting. Instead, after two days of this unique kind of convention, I found myself wondering why my family was not there with me. I had encountered love, the God I was searching for.

While driving on the way back home, I kept a deep silence, which was quite a contrast to the exuberance of my companions. One of them thought that I was either sick or that something was bothering me.

"What's going on with you?" And the other added, "Tell us, what happened to you?" I simply answered, "Oh, nothing," though there really was something that was eating away at me. I could not recall one thing that I listened to, not a thing. I was not able to focus in on anything that I may have heard or understood. Sure, some things I did understand, but applying them to my life was something altogether different.

A few days later I met Father Venanzio. "How is it going, Miguel?" "Not too good." And he, "Oh, then everything is o.k.!" "How can everything be o.k. if I can't remember anything I learned." Father broke into a hearty laugh and then smiled. I looked at him with surprise, thinking that he would have explained it to me. . . . Instead, he remarked, "God wants that you understand only what you need to understand, and that you recall only what you need to recall."

It was then that I really began to experience love and to understand. I felt an enormous joy. With whom could I possibly share it? My wife? My children? I spoke about these things with my friends at the tavern. Naturally, they thought that I was going crazy. After a while, I realized that I was fooling myself to no end; I wanted to get back to the way I was before. I could only say to myself, "Either you let go of everything or you just cannot continue on." The Word of Life that I had begun to meditate upon rang clearly: the old yeast that Paul refers to had to be cast away; I needed to be reborn in Christ. Was I capable of doing so? In the experience I had made in the midst of an authentic

Christian community joined together by the new commandment, I had discovered that only God could satisfy the human heart. I, too, understood that he is Love and that as his son, I decided that I, too, could in some way be "love." To be so, however, I really had to change.

It was not a matter of taking off to some place who knows where; I had to cut radically from my life of before, put God in the first place, and let everything else fall behind.

And yet, there was something absurd lurking in the air, a mysterious irony: my wife was showing opposition to my change, my whole household was against my new way of being. But why? Before, they wanted me to change, and now . . . It was like finding myself up against a strange and unexpected wall. I felt that I wasn't going to succeed. Full of anguish, but trustful, I turned to God: "Lord, if you are what is most important, the center of my life, everything else is secondary to me, my wife included, my father included, my children, everything."

Little by little, I began to notice a change in my wife. When we were at peace with one another, and happy, everything seemed to go in harmonious fashion, and this, I understood well, was the effect of unity. It was the presence of Jesus among us. My friends had told me this many times. We must love one another (therefore, my wife and I) to the point that Jesus can be in our midst, as he promised "Where two or three are gathered in my name, there am I in the midst of them" (Mt 18:20). What I tried to do, together with my wife, was to "put Jesus in our midst" so that he could unite us. On the other hand, when we had a disagreement, I don't know . . . it felt as though Jesus was no longer there, and that I had lost everything. This scared me. I was afraid to fall back into my former lifestyle.

One terrible night, we wound up in a heated discussion. I remembered in that moment that the only thing to save was the presence of Jesus among us, and so I fled for safety: "Listen, Rosa," and she interrupted, "I don't want to know about it." It was late, so we prepared for sleep. But I mentioned once again, "Listen, Rosa," and I heard once again, "I don't want to know anything from you." I felt destroyed. It was not only my wife I was losing, but I was losing Jesus. I thought, "If I lose Jesus in this moment, everything is over. I've lost it all." Nothing else mattered to me. I woke up only a few hours later; I had slept poorly. Rosa, too, was awake. I made another try at reestablishing our unity, but she continued to close up within herself. Fearfully thinking that this time for sure it was all over with, I abruptly got up, dressed, and went down to the living room. On the way I heard her following me. It's hard to say, maybe she had the intuition that I was at the end of my rope. I don't know. It was then that I hastily grabbed a book of Chiara Lubich off the shelf and told my wife: "Listen, Rosa, I want to show you why it is so important to me that we are united and that if we are not, why I am so afraid. If we are not united, everything is all over with, because I lose it all, I lose Jesus." We read together the meditation: "If we are united, Jesus is among us. This is what has true value. It is worth more than any other treasure that our hearts could possess: more than our mother, our father, our brothers and sisters, our children . . . more than our very own soul." I felt that we were again reunited, and that Rosa had chosen the same ideal.

*Rosa:* When last year Father Venanzio invited Miguel and me to a meeting of a religious nature, I couldn't understand why. But since he insisted, I talked it over with my daughters and we agreed: "Let's send our father and see what happens; let's do everything possible to convince him to go."

In fact, at that time I thought that he was the one at fault, he the one who was offending me, he who was betraying me. I felt that I was in the right; I was the obedient one, the victim who complied. I would even wait for his return in the evening, already prepared with what I had to say after listening to his apologies. I felt deserving to be the one to hear the apologies. When he came back from that meeting, I began to see a change in him. "How wonderful," I thought, "now that he has changed everything will go all right." And I simply sat back and waited for everything to change and to go well; I was the one in the right, there was nothing else for me to do!

Now, Miguel was coming home to have lunch each day; he was praying; he was reading the Bible; he was reading it to us . . . My daughters and I would look at each other: "Here he is with his stories again," and we would walk off into another room. One day, one of my daughters finally asked me, "How long is all this going to last?" Then, I spoke to her saying, "I spent all these years asking God for a change in your father and now that he has answered my requests, after twenty-eight years of marriage, I am the one who is rejecting him, I the one who refuses to be accepting of him. God listened to me, and who knows, this may be the last chance I have." My daughter was left speechless.

Several months had passed by: July, August, September. October 5th was Miguel's birthday. At home we got together and decided to celebrate by preparing a special meal, a gift, songs, a festive atmosphere to make him happy. However, on the day before Miguel said to me, "Listen, Rosa, if you are thinking of making me happy by preparing a party and a gift, I really don't want anything. But if you really want to make me happy, come with me and bring the children to a Word of Life meeting."[1] We accepted only to make him happy. For months afterwards, I even continued to accompany him to these meetings. He would say, "let's go here . . . let's go there," and I would follow him around.

I read the Words of Life, but immediately forgot them. He would bring up the issue, and I would respond by saying that I had already read it. One day, however, I read the current Word of Life and it struck me very forcefully. It spoke of "building peace." To build peace? How could I possibly build peace, if I myself were so torn to pieces inside, so full of anger, miserable and self-centered? I began to recall the events of my entire life. When in the past Miguel would upset me, I never took it silently. I would lash back at him in a very hard way. I began to remember all the remarks I had made to him over the years. The months that followed were extremely difficult for me. I was very ill-at-ease. My memories were killing me. During the course of these twenty-eight years, I had listened to Miguel's apologies, but never once had I apologized to him. This was the only thing that remained on my mind. I looked for the right moment, but when meeting him I could not speak up. I felt it was my pride that kept me from uttering just a few simple words: "forgive me." I had many chances, but I was unable to take advantage of them. Finally, on the day before a scheduled meeting for families, Miguel approached me and suggested, "You know, we could share our experience." I remember that my anger rose at that moment and I responded by saying that I had nothing to tell to anyone and that he should not coax me into doing it. However,

---

1. A small reunion of families, young people, and other members of the Focolare movement where the experience of living the gospel in one's own daily life is shared.

at the meeting the following day, though I feared to speak in front of so many people, with a mind that felt so empty, I turned to God and said, "You know what I will say. I don't. Please help me." I will always be thankful to God. It turned out to be the greatest and most wonderful day of my life. While speaking to everyone, I was finally able to ask Miguel to forgive me. I felt on that day that I was reborn with a new and true love. Before then, I had tried to love my husband with only a human love. I saw him only as a man, not as a son of God, as another Jesus.

The Word of Life was changing me within; I felt as though the old yeast was breaking apart. I began to truly believe that Miguel and I were at least on our way to living with the mentality of Jesus.

*M. and R. S.*
*(Mexico)*

# 7.
# *The Greatest Work*

*"I solemnly assure you, the man who has faith in me will do the works I do, and greater far than these. Why? Because I go to the Father"* (Jn 14:12).

This seems to be one of the most astonishing statements of Jesus: how can his disciples do works of his degree or even greater ones than these? Hadn't Jesus during his life, as we read in the gospels, performed miracle after miracle? Had he not even gone so far as to raise the dead?

Perhaps we can better understand what he is saying by studying what is meant here by "far greater" works.

But let's go in order.

It is the eve of his passion. During the Last Supper, among the sublime things that he says and works in order to prepare the disciples all the way to the end, he also speaks about his unity with the Father, so evident in his works. At this point he affirms:

*"I solemnly assure you, the man who has faith in me will do the works I do, and greater far than these. Why? Because I go to the Father."*

Jesus opens this statement with the words "I solemnly assure you." By doing so he announces the importance and the depth of what he is about to say.

Then he immediately refers to "the man who has faith": not only, therefore, to the disciples present or to some privileged souls, but to each and every Christian. The person who believes in Christ, the one who is united to him and who lives of his life, is in the position to do works as his, and furthermore, will do greater ones.

As we can see, Jesus does not mean here any action whatsoever, but rather those that he performs; that is, in continuation with those that he has already done, so as to reopen to humankind communion with the Father, so as to communicate to all people his salvation.

This does not mean that the disciples will be greater than their Master, because through their actions, it is Jesus himself who, even after his return to the Father, continues to act within the world.

*"I solemnly assure you, the man who has faith in me will do the works I do, and greater far than these. Why? Because I go to the Father."*

As far as the "greater" works, which Jesus will accomplish through those who believe in him, we can think of the miracles performed by the disciples, the conversions that occurred by means of their preaching that were of greater number than those converted while Jesus had spoken; or of the proclamation of the gospel by Christians throughout the entire world, while Jesus himself remained within the confines of Palestine. The greatness of these works, however, certainly do not lie in their exterior aspect, in their number, or in their geographical extension.

The "far greater" works consist essentially in giving to others the life that is divine, the power of the Holy Spirit, and therefore, adoption as children of God. Jesus obtained this in its fullness only in his death and resurrection. He will communicate this life, therefore, after his glorious transfiguration: and he will be able to do so through the works of his disciples.

Jesus says, in fact: "Because I go to the Father." Jesus' departure does not interrupt his work of the salvation of the world, but assures its growth and its expansion; his departure is not a separation from those who were close to him, but a real, though invisible presence of himself within them. It is their unity with he who is Risen that makes them capable of performing "greater works," of reuniting the people of the earth with the Father and among themselves.

*"I solemnly assure you, the man who has faith in me will do the works I do, and greater far than these. Why? Because I go to the Father."*

How can we live this Word of Life?

It depends on us whether Jesus will pass onto this earth today and accomplish his work: he acts through us, if we let him do so.

Even for the first time he came to earth, God asked Mary, one of us, for her consent. Mary believed: she adhered totally to the Father's plans. What "work" did her faith produce? Because of her yes, "the Word became flesh" (Jn 1:14) in her and the salvation of humankind was made possible.

We, too, have a great responsibility: we must believe in Jesus so that he might live in us and work through us. We must welcome and put into practice his words, which find their synthesis in the new commandment. Let's forget ourselves and set out to love others as he loved, with a love that knows no measure. Out of the tomb of our ego, the risen Lord, with his power, his light, and his joy, will live in a greater way each day within each one of us and in the midst of us.

The world has dire need of his presence. May this be our "work," our "greater work": to live in such a way as to offer to all those we meet the risen Lord alive in us and among us. In him much of humanity will find what outside of him can only be sought for in vain: hope, goodness, truth, unity, peace. With him we will work for the true transformation of the world.

*Chiara Lubich*

## *A treatment of mutual love*

I work for a Rehabilitation Center where counties place fourteen- to eighteen-year-old young men who have committed such crimes as burglary, arson, rape, theft, and robbery. My job as a counselor and supervisor of other counselors is to help these young men to stop their anti-social behaviors so that they can return to the world without endangering others, and hopefully, so that they can even become contributing members of their communities.

On my second day of work, violence erupted. One student, convinced that everyone was against him, kicked one counselor in the shoulder and kicked another in the mouth, cursing and yelling furiously. To restrain him, I struggled with him for about four hours. I left at five in the afternoon with my shirt in shreds, bruised and shaken. The fighting continued well into the night.

Although things like this only happened about once a month, on most days staff went to work nervous, since they knew an eruption could happen any time. The atmosphere was always tense. For the most part, order was maintained with abusive language and physical threats. Fist fights and wrestling matches between staff and students were not uncommon. Group therapy sessions were usually just an opportunity for strong students to verbally abuse weaker students. One staff person sold students their own cigarettes for one dollar apiece. Another allowed students to be out in the community totally unsupervised. Some slept on the job. Some enforced what they called "group sanctions," where the whole group had to pay for one student's mistake. After giving the punishment, staff would leave the room, knowing the other students would then beat up the one who had made the mistake. In a disagreement with students, staff people never admitted they were wrong. They also often criticized one another in public, saying the other was weak, since what was important was to be tough.

In the beginning I too believed staff had to fight with students every so often, just to show them who was stronger. After I became the supervisor I even suggested that staff take martial arts classes to gain respect. Once I got my own nose smashed in a sparring match, believing it was important to show I was "street tough." I really thought it was necessary to be ready and willing to fight to maintain order.

In short, it was a pretty miserable environment to work in and an even worse environment to be sentenced to if you had broken the law.

A couple of years ago I attended a gathering where I heard a psychologist speak about his treatment of young children with mental health problems. His ideas were based on mutual love. He gave me the outline he was using in his treatment, but said I would have to apply it in my own situation. I went back to my job convinced that my work environment could change. Using his ideas, I made a model for our students, telling them to try a four-step method, which was a practical application of the concept of mutual love, to become sure of their mental health. I explained how they would be able to see their best selves in action and to help others become their best selves.

Morning meetings have always been a part of our treatment program. They used to be an opportunity for one student to tell another that he was angry, or that the other was doing something wrong. In order to keep the meeting from turning into an argument, the student being addressed was not allowed to respond. However, I thought this meeting could do a lot more good. As supervisor, I changed the agenda to also include what they have done right. (Now they remember what good the other does, and they tell it to each other at these morning meetings.)

At the same time, I started trying to serve the students and my fellow workers. I began helping students with their chores. I carried chairs, ran the vacuum and cleaned the commode with them. I try to do everything I can to get them clothes when they need them. Sometimes they arrive with only a few clothes in a garbage bag. Getting them some more clothes involves a lot of red tape and I try to get through it as quickly as possible. I also publicly recognize and commend students when they help one another.

I also began looking for opportunities to serve the other staff members. I visited one in the hospital a couple of times. This helped build a better relationship. To help my boss, who has difficulty organizing things, I write weekly plans. One counselor has poor writing skills so I rewrite his reports trying not to complain. Another's boyfriend went to jail, and I listen to her talk about this stressful situation.

As the supervisor of the facility, I've written letters commending staff when they have shown care and concern for the students, other staff, or the program as a whole. I send copies of these recognition letters to three different administrators and also to the staff person's permanent personnel folder. This increases our unity and also encourages staff to continue these acts of service.

As a result of these new relationships at work, staff and students began to join me in this new approach. There have been fruits in every aspect of life at the facility.

For example, staff and students are recognizing the need for a mutual communion of goods. Members of the staff often bring clothes in from home to give to the students. Recently, I discovered that I wasn't using a nice winter bathrobe, so I took it to work and gave it to a student. A couple of days later another student gave me a nice shirt that really looks good on me. He said his father gave it ho him, but it really wasn't his style, and I would look much better in it. I really like the shirt.

One staff member volunteered to teach a Bible study to students on Saturday mornings, when the students usually sleep late. Five of them said "yes."

When one of our teacher's aides was recently in the hospital, two of the students made get-well cards, all the others signed them and two students and a staff person visited her.

Our students are ordered to spend nine months to a year at our facility. Because they are dangerous, some are brought to the facility wearing handcuffs and shackles. You wouldn't think they'd care about the way this "lock-up center" looked.

Recently, however, we had to give the facility a good thorough cleaning because the Department of Public Welfare was coming for an inspection. Because of this relationship of mutual cooperation between the staff and students, the students put long hours into cleaning the whole facility. They knew it was really a staff concern and not theirs, but they helped us. We worked together scrubbing everything from garbage cans to the oven. We all had a sense of pride about how the facility looked when the inspector arrived.

Many of our students who have completed the program still call us to let us know how well they're doing or because they need help. About six months ago a student called to say there are good Alcoholics Anonymous meetings at the church he attends, which is close enough to our facility that our students could also attend. Since he was getting a lot out of the meetings he wanted to help the others.

The facility hardly seems like the same place it was the day I left with my shirt torn and the violence continuing into the night. In fact, one student who used to steal cars and trade them for cocaine, recently told another. "You have to realize that using drugs and all the money you get from selling drugs is worth nothing. Caring about people is the only thing that counts."

*M. M.*

# 8.
# Believing in Mercy

*"God did not send the Son into the world to condemn the world, but that the world might be saved through him"* (Jn 3:17).

In biblical language, the verb "to judge" has the same meaning as to "to condemn."

The Word of Life tells us, therefore, that God did not send his Son in order to condemn the world, but so that, through him, the world might be saved.

We have before us a statement immensely rich in significance. Jesus reveals to us the true face of God, that he is love, and that the most moving aspect of his love is his mercy. Love was the driving force for which the Father sent his Son into the world; through the life of Jesus, we touch the Father's boundless love. It is a love that seeks out his creatures, that always awaits their return, that looks beyond all their faults, and that forgives and saves.

It is enough to recall certain marvelous episodes of the gospel, which demonstrate to us Jesus' love for sinners (Zaccheus, the adulteress, and so on) or the parables that indicate his mercy (the prodigal son).

*"God did not send the Son into the world to condemn the world, but that the world might be saved through him."*

In order to better understand these words of Jesus, it would be useful to consider the verse that appears immediately before this one. It reads: "God so loved the world that he gave his only Son, that whoever believes in him may not die but may have eternal life" (Jn 3:16).

"Whoever believes in him . . ."

The infinite love of God expects then our reply: that we believe in his Son, that we believe that Jesus welcomes us back with open arms when we sincerely repent for having offended him through our sins, that we might return to him, believing in his mercy.

*"God did not send the Son into the world to condemn the world, but that the world might be saved through him."*

There are different ways today to lose sight of God's mercy. The first way, unfortunately very widespread, is that of no longer recognizing the reality of sin, and that of our own sinfulness. Without recognizing ourselves as sinners, we can no longer sense any need for the Savior, just as when we don't recognize that we are ill, we don't feel the need to see a doctor. Such an attitude necessarily blocks the way to Jesus' mercy, who came not for those who claim to be righteous and self-sufficient, but for those who recognize themselves as sinners and who are incapable of doing good without his help (cf. Lk 5:31-32).

We can lose sight of God's mercy also by not believing in it with full assurance.

Many Christians believe in God's mercy because they learned of it in their catechisms, but their belief has remained only on a conceptual or intellectual level and thus has not been able to penetrate their everyday lives. All kinds of reasoning, perhaps, can enclose us within ourselves with a feeling of regret as we ponder over our sins. Moreover, our reasoning might be more a reflection of our pride than of our sorrow for having offended God, which leaves us in a state of discouragement. All this goes to show that we are relying more on ourselves than on the infinite mercy of Jesus and on the power of his grace. Instead, to believe in divine mercy means to be wholeheartedly convinced that if we ask to be forgiven, Jesus will completely cancel out our sins, and with this it means that we get up immediately and follow him.

*"God did not send the Son into the world to condemn the world, but that the world might be saved through him."*

Therefore, how can we live this Word of Life?

We must concretely and beyond all limits believe in the mercy of Jesus; we must give him the gift of our nothingness each time our shortcomings and weaknesses give us the chance to do so, convinced that this gift—if accompanied by the decision to begin again—is not a superficial gesture, but an act of pure love that attracts his forgiveness and grace. Further, we must be convinced that this would be the most beautiful response we could give to his love.

Jesus' mercy extends out to us in a particular way through the sacraments, especially the sacraments of reconciliation and the eucharist. We should, therefore, make always better use of the sacrament of reconciliation by opening our hearts with ever greater simplicity, without any fear or shame, as though we were truly in front of Jesus. We must also try to approach the sacrament of the eucharist always more conscious of what we are doing.

In fact, one of the effects of the eucharist—if we receive it with the desire to grow in the love that Jesus taught us—is precisely that of purifying us of all the imperfections and the effects of sin, which we fall into every day.

*"God did not send the Son into the world to condemn the world, but that the world might be saved through him."*

The gospel says: "I tell you, there will likewise be more joy in heaven over one repentant sinner than over ninety-nine righteous people who have no need to repent" (Lk 15:7).

Wouldn't it be the case for all of us, sinners as we always are, to return over and over again into the arms of God's mercy, also as a way to send to God a bit of joy from this earth? For a world so torn to pieces by thousands of evils and dangers, here and there already at the mercy of war and threatened by atomic outbursts, couldn't this be a way to draw down God's blessings?

*Chiara Lubich*

## *Anthony's story*

As I was leaving my girlfriend's house late one evening in Manhattan, I saw from a distance what looked to be a friend's little brother. I wasn't sure because the kid looked like a drug addict. I thought it couldn't be him and I just continued walking. When I got to the corner, however, somebody called my name. I turned around and saw that it was he. His features had changed a lot but I recognized his eyes.

I wanted to just try to love him, but I was so disappointed to see him in that state. He was only seventeen at the time. I took him to get something to eat. We talked but he never looked me in the eyes. I kept staring at him to be sure it was really Anthony because my disbelief was just so heavy.

When we separated that night, I gave him my phone number without really expecting to hear from him again. I said, "If you need a friend to talk to, I'm here for you."

Sure enough about two weeks later, at three o'clock in the morning, the phone rang and it was he. At first I was annoyed, but then I thought he was smoking a lot of crack and they usually stay up at night and sleep during the day. I thought if I want to love him I have to kind of punch his time clock and be there when he's available. So, I put on my clothes and I went to Manhattan and we sat and talked over something to eat.

He started calling me regularly. It was hard because I was working for a stock brokerage firm at the time and there was a lot of pressure involved with my job, but I still made it through the day. The relationship started to grow and one day he asked me, "Are you smoking crack? Because every time I call, you always come out? What's the story?" I started telling him how I had changed my life, how I had started to meet with other young people who like me try to live the gospel in their daily lives, especially the aspect of unity (see Jn 17). He was interested in learning how to build unity. He told me about how his relationship with his mother had fallen apart at home. His older brother had moved away and all his mother wanted to do was talk about God and save his soul. This was a turnoff to him. Plus he was stealing a lot of things from the house and sometimes he wasn't allowed back in. There was a lot of disunity there. I started explaining to him how the Gospel was a way of life that applied to his situation. I told him how also Jesus suffered on the cross and how he could give his suffering and failures to God out of love. It really clicked with him.

He would stop getting high for a week or two and then he would go on a binge for a couple of days. Then he would stop again. But he improved tremendously; he was really making a big effort. The rehabilitation centers that he had gone to before never really worked because with crack, it's really up to you. Then he decided that he wanted to start receiving the sacraments again: go to confession and receive communion. I took him to church with me.

After a while, it seemed like he had surpassed me in trying to live the gospel.

In the past, he was considered dangerous because he was always out in the streets, always fighting and he wouldn't mind busting somebody's head to get their money. All of a sudden he was straightening out.

In the beginning of our relationship, I was always correcting him: "Anthony don't talk so loud, don't always talk slang, don't use all that profanity . . ." Now he even got himself an honest little job in a store. He would come home on pay day, and when the bums would ask him for money, he would give it to them. The other kids caught on and tried to take advantage of him but he didn't put up a fight, he just gave them his money out of love. That was a hard thing to do because when you're living in the streets, the basic thing is that you have to be tough because people will always be after you.

There were these two guys who were after him for his money, and they were about my age. I thought it was my civic duty to humble them, you know. So one day we were coming up out of the train station, and I said, "Let's walk down 46th street." Anthony didn't want to because he knew the two guys would be there. We were walking up the block and saw the two guys coming towards us and I was saying in my mind, "Maybe this is the will of God that they're here." Very sure of myself I said: "Anthony, just let me handle this." But I was already so mad and my blood pressure had already elevated that my profound words quickly turned into angry words and before I knew it we were in a little brawl. After it was over, Anthony gave the guys his money and said he was very disappointed in me. "How could you do that," he asked, "and be a Christian and go to church every Sunday?" He made me feel really terrible.

The following Sunday we went to church and while I sat in the back, Anthony went to confession. Since it was my parish I knew the parishioners that were there. Anthony came out and sat next to me and said: "Well, Martin, don't you have something to confess?" I still felt terrible about the brawl but I said, "Okay, I'll go." The priest had left the confessional and was leaving the church. Anthony started to call him: "Wait, there's another one! The big guy is coming by." I was very embarrassed but I couldn't get mad because he did it so innocently.

Anthony was really doing well and we had become really strong friends. I had tried to bring Christ to him and I received so much in return.

One day Anthony's mother called to say that he had died during the night. I think it was because the drugs had ruined his health. Some kids had chased him home. He ran into the house, kissed his mother and told her he was going straight to sleep. She told me that he was breathing very heavily and was out of breath. When she went to wake him up in the morning he had passed away. But I think he's safe in God because one of the things he would often repeat to me was: "Martin, I want to be good; I want to have peace in my life." He had found it so quickly that he was able to teach me.

*G. M.*

# 9.
# Before the Eyes of Those Around Us

*"Whoever acknowledges me before men I will acknowledge before my Father in heaven. Whoever disowns me before men I will disown before my Father in heaven"* (Mt 10:32-33).

This is a word which offers great comfort and incentive for all of our lives as Christians.

Here Jesus earnestly advises us to live in coherence with our faith in him, because our eternal destiny depends on the attitude we have assumed in his regard during our earthly lives. If we will have acknowledged him before the eyes of those around us, we will give him reason to acknowledge us before his Father; if, on the contrary, we will have disowned him before the world, he too will disown us before the Father.

*"Whoever acknowledges me before men I will acknowledge before my Father in heaven. Whoever disowns me before men I will disown before my Father in heaven."*

Jesus calls attention to the reward or the punishment that awaits us after this life, because he loves us. He knows, as a father of the Church tells us, that at times fear of punishment is more effective than a beautiful promise. For this reason he increases our hope for eternal happiness and at the same time, in order to save us, he instills in us the fear of condemnation.

What matters to him is that we come to live forever with God. Besides, it is the only thing that counts; it is the end for which we have been given life: only with him, in fact, will we attain our complete fulfillment, the satisfaction of all our aspirations. This is why Jesus urges us to "acknowledge him" already here on earth. If instead we don't want to have anything to do with him in this life, if we disown him now, when it becomes time to pass on to the next life, we will find ourselves separated from him forever.

At the end of our earthly journey, therefore, Jesus will do no other than confirm before the Father the choice each one of us had made on earth, with all of its consequences. In referring to the final judgement, he makes us aware of the great importance and the seriousness of the decision we make here below: in reality, what is at play is our eternal life.

*"Whoever acknowledges me before men I will acknowledge before my Father in heaven. Whoever disowns me before men I will disown before my Father in heaven."*

How can we take advantage of this warning of Jesus? How can we live this word of his?

He tells us himself: "Whoever acknowledges me . . ."

Let's decide then to acknowledge him before others with simplicity and frankness.

Let's overcome human respect. Let's move out of our mediocrity and our compromises, which empty even our Christian lives of their authenticity.

Let's keep in mind that we are called to be witnesses to Christ: he wants to reach all people with his message of peace, of justice, of love, precisely through us.

Let's give witness to him wherever we are, whether it be in the family, at work, in our friendships, our studies or in any of life's circumstances.

Let's bear witness above all through our example, through a life lived in honesty, with detachment from money, modesty in our dress, sharing the joys and sorrows of others.

Let's bear witness to Christ in a special way through our reciprocal love, our unity, so that the peace and true joy Jesus promises to those united to him may fill our spirits already here on earth and be extended to others.

To whomever might ask why we live in such a way, why we maintain such serenity amidst a world so afflicted, let's respond then, in humility and sincerity with the words the Holy Spirit will suggest to us. In this way we will bear witness to Christ also through our words, also on the plane of concepts and ideas.

Perhaps, then, many of those who are searching for him will be able to find him.

At times we will be misunderstood and contradicted; we will be disliked, made fun of, and persecuted. Jesus has warned us ahead of time: "They persecuted me, they will persecute you" (Jn 15:20).

We are on the right road. Let's continue then to courageously bear witness to him even in the midst of trials, even at the cost of our life. The goal that awaits us is worth the price. It is heaven, where Jesus, whom we love, will acknowledge us before the Father for the rest of eternity.

*Chiara Lubich*

## *A difficult witness*

Abortion is legal in our country, and the people consider it a very normal procedure. We have reached the point that the number of abortions far surpasses the number of babies born.

I am a nurse. One day, the administration of the various gynecological wards of the hospital where I work unanimously accepted the proposal for a new set of guidelines. When we were told that we were expected to assist in performing this practice, I was left in shock. I had no intention to back down on my convictions, thus I was ready to refuse and accept what would be the consequences. I remember that I immediately let my husband and children know I could very soon be let go from my job.

With this in mind, I publicly opposed such an imposition and highlighted the reason for which our ward was built: to defend life.

I had everyone against me. They knew my action stemmed from my religious beliefs, and this fueled even further their rejection. The director severely reproved me and threatened to commit me to the disciplinary board. For me, however, what was important was to live the word of the gospel: "Whoever acknowledges me before men I will acknowledge before my Father in heaven."

The following day, to my surprise, some of the nurses stated that they would follow my line of thought. The majority, however, continued to belittle me and accuse me of being old-fashioned. It was a very difficult moment, but as always I drew my strength from the gospel. I remembered the words of Jesus, "If anyone comes to me without turning his back on his father and mother, his wife and his children, his brothers and sisters, indeed his very self, he cannot be my follower." Soon afterwards, several other colleagues gave me their support and the number continued to grow until the night before the new directives were scheduled to take effect. By this time, I was astonished to realize that almost our entire working force was against this new procedure. Even the head of our ward came to the conclusion that it was absurd to see that in the same ward there were people who took measures to safeguard life, while at the same time others who took part in destroying life. Five years have gone by since then, and this issue is now only a thing of the past. . . .

There are continuous cases that surface, however, where it is determined that the mother's pregnancy places her in serious danger and the doctors decide on abortion.

I have felt more than ever that my place is to be at the mothers' side to encourage them to save their child at all costs. I recall the case of a patient who had a grave heart condition. Three times while she was under care, the doctors, fearing the worst, wanted to resort to abortion. When I realized, however, that the woman, even though very fearful still wanted to keep the baby, I advised her to take the risk and I assured her that I would attend to her all the way to birth. This was so encouraging to her, that notwithstanding her tears, she pronounced her decision to the commission.

They tried to dissuade her, but it was enough that we glanced at one another to give her the strength to go against everyone else.

Her hospital stay was a long one, but she gave birth to a beautiful daughter. Her happiness was indescribable. . .

Another woman, whose pregnancy was at an advanced stage, needed to undergo a risky surgery involving her spinal column. The doctors considered it more than logical to terminate her pregnancy. I didn't know what to do, but I took advantage of each free moment I had to run over to see her. I prayed that God would enlighten me. At a certain point, trusting in the strength of the relationship that grew among us, I advised her to postpone the operation. Even though the doctors had a contrary view point, given the seriousness of her individual case, she placed her trust in me, and with trembling hand affirmed that she would assume the responsibility of that decision. During the remaining months I tried to stay as close to her as possible. One way I found to assist her was to understand that since she was Moslem, she could not eat all the food that the hospital indicated for her. I often prepared food for her at home and would bring it to work with me. It was the head nurse who later gave word to the kitchen to prepare her a diet that was coherent with her faith.

Each day that passed brought increasing hope that she would proceed well all the way to the birth. In fact, she bore a healthy child. Those most astonished were the doctors. One of them confessed to have never come across a case as such in any kind of manual. The head of the ward went as far as to comment: "Who knows whether this is really a scientific fact or whether God has in some way intervened."

Something similar happened to a woman under treatment for a grave kidney disease. It was also decided for her that she should terminate her pregnancy. Together we hoped and we pleaded with the doctors to wait. Several days went by and the new kidney tests showed a significant improvement. The doctors, fearing an error in recording, had the tests repeated three different times. In any case, she finally gave birth by caesarean section to a healthy baby. It was hard to believe that the mother had only one kidney, and a damaged one at that.

One day I was called to the telephone. The voice sounded very familiar, but at that moment I could not recognize who it was. She introduced herself as a woman who on several occasions was treated in my ward. She now wanted to talk to me about her tragedy: she was expecting a fourth child, but because of her financial condition she felt she could not keep it.

I went to visit her in order to get a better grasp of her situation. Her husband was also home; they had already decided to have the abortion. All the same, I tried to explain to her how every life belongs to God and we cannot destroy it. . . . Conscious as they already were of this, they still could not see any other alternative. I returned back home with a lump in my throat. Looking to the crucifix hanging in the room, I realized that this new situation was also a reflection of his infinite suffering.

On the day of the operation, the telephone rang: she was in bed with the flu and her operation was rescheduled for the following week. We kept in touch by phone during the week and one day she called to joyfully announce that she and her husband had decided to keep the baby.

Another similar case was that of a woman who was expecting her seventh child; she, too, due to economic difficulties, felt she could not continue her pregnancy. However, it was enough that I offered her my assistance, financially speaking as well, that she found the determination to bring her child into the world. The decision cost her many battles with her family, but she held up due to the strength she received from our relationship. She, too, gave birth to a beautiful baby boy. At the same moment, she was surrounded by the concrete love of other families who, to the surprise of her parents, smothered him with gifts.

Still another case. One day I was to substitute for a colleague of mine in another ward. My task was to assist the patients already scheduled for terminating their pregnancies. A woman arrived with her daughter. I was struck to see how frightened the daughter was, and how nervous was her mother who didn't leave her alone for a second. I arranged things so that I could talk personally with the daughter in another room. I asked her if she wanted to keep her child. She burst out crying; it was her mother and the rest of the family who insisted on the abortion.

I spoke to her about the life she carried within her, about her being already a mother, even though the baby was just conceived. She calmed down and became convinced that she would give birth to the baby she already loved.

When we went back outside, her mother caused a great scene in front of everyone. She then left the hospital, leaving her daughter behind. I remained with the daughter, promising her my own support and the support of other friends of mine.

Now, the whole family is actually waiting joyfully for the daughter's baby to arrive, including the mother, who changed her point of view and looks forward to nothing else than to become a grandmother.

In the town where I live, people often come to me for advice concerning abortion or they seek explanations on hospital care. Many are teenage mothers who don't know how to break the news to their parents.

In cases as such, I challenge them to face the situation. I recall even the case of a forty-three year-old unmarried woman whose parents were old and very sick. After the long and repeated talks we had together, she decided to keep the baby.

The most striking experience for me of all, however, occurred when I returned to work after a week's vacation. An abortion was performed on a woman late in pregnancy. The head nurse, who assisted the procedure, was literally shaken from witnessing that the extracted baby remained alive for another two hours.

"The baby's crying was making me go insane," she confided

to me, "and so I did what you often do . . . so that at least up there he might have what he lacked here." She was not a believer, but she repeated the words of a baptismal rite that she heard me pronounce on various occasions while also calling the baby by a Christian name.

*J. K.*
*(Yugoslavia)*

## 10.
# A Trap Set by Love

*"We know that God makes all things work together for the good of those who love him"* (Rom 8:28).

In order to understand better such a marvelous phrase as this, one that will never cease to shed light on the events that shape our lives, we need to read it in the context of St. Paul's writings, which reveal God's love for all.

In Paul's letter, in fact, we often encounter the theme of God's love for us and his grace, which immensely surpass every weakness of ours: God has a plan of love for us. He has had us in mind from all eternity. He created us. His call consists in reproducing the image of his Son in us (cf. Rom 8:29; Eph 1:4). The sending of his Son into the world and the gift of his Spirit give us the assurance that the Father will do everything possible in order to bring his plan to completion, leaving nothing untried (cf. Rom 8:32, 8:15-17). He makes all things work together for the good of those who love him. It is what the word we meditate upon affirms:

*"We know that God makes all things work together for the good of those who love him."*

". . . of those who love God."

Not for everyone, therefore, does everything work for

the good, but for those who love God and they are the ones who respond to his love. God's love for each one of us is not of a generic kind, but a love that is personal and special. He makes everything work for the good — that is, for the salvation, true happiness, and spiritual progress — of those who love him.

*"We know that God makes all things work together for the good of those who love him."*

"All things . . ."

Everything. Therefore, he refers not only to his word, or to the sacraments or ministries, or to any other means he has given to the Church for our spiritual good. All those things would be evident.

The apostle Paul means something more: for those who believe in the love of God and love him, the most varied circumstances that condition one's existence are not seen as simply dictated by chance or by the blind laws of nature, but they are all guided by this love. They are occasions and means by which God serves to bring his work of sanctification to completion. He conceals himself behind all the events of one's life, a given health condition for example, or some particular cause for disappointment, an unexpected change in program due to a new set of circumstances; he lies behind the particular state of life one has set out on, a sudden trial of a moral nature, or any kind of difficulty found at work. He hides himself behind the fact that we find ourselves to be at a specific place, next to a specific person. Everything, for the one who loves God, even the very mistakes of the past, acquires positive meaning, because through all these circumstances, one can experience the love of God who wants to guide us toward sanctity.

*"We know that God makes all things work together for the good of those who love him."*

However, we can become aware of God's loving direction for us only inasmuch as we love him; that is, inasmuch as we abandon ourselves to him, convinced that his thoughts are not our own and that our salvation and our complete Christian fulfillment pass through ways that do not always coincide with our own.

If, on the other hand, we do not place our trust in him, we will not be able to see and experience God's love for us hidden behind all of life's events.

We must also keep in mind that to believe in God's love does not mean to be fatalistic in entrusting to him the solution of our problems. It means struggling to overcome sickness, suffering, injustice, and evils of every form and kind.

The balance found in Christian life, in fact, consists in uniting a filial abandon to what God wishes for us together with our own personal initiative.

*"We know that God makes all things work together for the good of those who love him."*

How then, can we live this Word of Life?

First of all, we must never view anything solely from an exterior or material point of view, but rather believe that all that happens carries a message, through which God expresses his love for us.

We will see how life itself, though it may appear to us as the opposite side of an embroidery design, full of knots and threads confusingly intertwined with one another, is really something quite different: it is the marvelous design that the love of God is weaving on the basis of our faith.

Secondly, we must totally and confidently abandon ourselves to this love in every passing moment, whether it be in small or big things. Moreover, if we learn to entrust ourselves to the love of God in life's more common circumstances, he will give us the strength to entrust ourselves to him in the more difficult moments, which can surface as a great trial, a serious sickness, or even the very moment of death itself.

Let's try then to live in this way, certainly not by seeking our personal gain, for example, so that God might manifest his plans to us or that he might give us consolation, but only out of love. We will see how this confident abandon in him is a source of infinite light and peace for us and for many others.

*Chiara Lubich*

## *My turn as gift*

It was a Monday morning following a weekend convention in upstate New York. I had stayed with friends in New Jersey Sunday evening and was travelling into Manhattan in order to return home to Houston, Texas that day. I was with a friend, and at the railway station we met a mutual friend. As we went into the station from the parking lot I felt some chest pain but for a few moments was undecided as to whether it was from the cold weather or if it was the angina pain related to the seventy percent blockage of one of my arteries.

I had known for two months that I had this heart difficulty and the doctor had me carry nitrostat tablets in case the pain occurred. I had not had to use it during the two-month period since my condition had been diagnosed. Immediately after buying my train ticket I decided that I was experiencing the angina pain so I took one of my tablets. There was no relief. Twice before I had experienced this pain and it had subsided on its own within a short time, so I boarded the crowded train.

Since the train was full we stood, but by then I was beginning to perspire profusely. I spotted an empty seat right inside the next railway car and went to it. I did not think of a heart attack but I realized that I needed medical attention. At that point, I told my friend how I felt and that I should get to a hospital emergency room as quickly as possible. He suggested we get off the train at the next stop, rather than proceed into New York City as planned, and I agreed.

At that point a woman who sat facing me had overheard our conversation and said: "I am a physician. I will tell the conductor to call ahead to Newark so that an ambulance can be there when we arrive." My discomfort was increasing and I placed myself in God's hands, praying that whatever was his will for me would be accomplished. Shortly after the lady physician left to speak to the conductor, a man came and sat with me saying he also was a physician and a cardiologist. He asked the persons seated across from me to get up so that I could lie down, and began taking my medical history, and asking about my medication. He kept his fingers on my pulse and spoke to me encouragingly.

I heard a person nearby say that he had the very same medication with him and did the doctor want to give me some since mine seemed to have no effect. The doctor advised him to do so. By this time, I was becoming less attentive to what was going on around me. I was aware that as we pulled into the Newark station the persons in the car were asked to step back and wait until the paramedic team had boarded and removed me by chair stretcher. The three-person team began immediately to minister to me while still on the train.

The physician who had stayed with me got off as well and gave the team the medical information he had gathered. I did not envy them the long flight of stairs they had to carry me down to the waiting ambulance. My two friends who were on their way to work in New York City accompanied me in the ambulance. Once in the emergency room, I responded to further questions but with increasing difficulty until I drifted off.

A few hours later I regained consciousness and found myself in a cardiac intensive care unit. I was hooked up to a monitor and counted six IV bags hanging over me. A doctor was standing beside me along with several medical students or residents. He told me I had survived a heart attack and that had I not been in the emergency room when I lost consciousness, I would be dead.

He continued to explain that I had been given a new drug, PTC, which until last January had been experimental. It had the effect of immediately clearing the blockage of the artery. As soon as I became sufficiently stabilized, I would be moved to a larger medical center where I would undergo a new medical procedure. This was done the following day and the result was that my previous 70 percent blockage was now reduced to thirty percent.

In the meantime my family began arriving. Rather than feeling any pain I was experiencing a profound sense of awe and gratitude to God for this incredible demonstration of how people can be instruments of his love. How could I not understand the presence on the same train of two doctors of which one was a cardiologist, and a person using my same medicine, as providence from God who makes all things work together for those who love him? It was obvious that my life was more than ever now his gift to be lived for him.

*D.J.*

## *Our blossomed marriage*

*Mary:* Sometimes I feel as if my life began only two years ago instead of thirty-one years before that. In these last two years our marriage has blossomed into something so beautiful that not even the greatest efforts of my imagination could have envisioned the results.

I was born into a wonderful family. All of my childhood was immersed in love. My parents are really special people who live a married love of joy. My brothers and sisters too are special people who envelop me with caring love. From them all I learned that love is the basis of everything — from it springs acceptance, forgiveness, the knowledge that people aren't perfect, the beauty of starting again, the fact that loving is giving and therefore full of joy.

One thing that I didn't realize for a long time was just how special this family was. In my naivety, I thought that most families were like ours, and that everyone knew about love. It was this blindness in me that stopped me seeing how to truly love.

I was eighteen when I met Bob, and, when we married three years later, I loved him to the limit of my capacity. I could see what a really special person he was, and I saw him then, as I still do now, as one of God's gifts to me. What I didn't see were the great hurts inside him. His background was superficially like mine, and so I assumed that he viewed the world as I did. I didn't recognize that, under the mask which his family held to the world, there were hurting people who knew only bitterness, hatred and resentment, who had only skills for self-protection, and who expected only exploitation and abuse. I didn't realize that, if people have never been loved, then they don't know how to recognize love and they don't know how to love. So it was with Bob.

And so it was that, in my ignorance of Bob's hurts, I managed to continually add to them. The little things that I said I heard with my ears and not with Bob's. When I said out of love, "Thanks for doing a great job mending that cupboard!" I didn't realize that he heard me say, "You're no good for anything except mending cupboards." When I suggested as an idea "Let's have a picnic on Sunday," I didn't know that he heard me saying "If we don't have a picnic on Sunday, I'll be in such a bad mood that you'll regret staying home." When I said (with a great effort of will!) "I'm sorry," what he heard was "I know you're wrong, and I'll prove that I'm a better person by showing good manners." Sometimes I wonder why he wanted to stay married to the unpleasant person he saw me to be!

Because I didn't know how to become one with Bob, because I didn't realize the necessity for becoming one with him, I didn't know how to love him.

As time went on, Bob began to react to me with violence. At first I was stunned. I examined myself closely. I felt that I really had to change myself if I was provoking him to hit me. So I tried. Each time, I tried to cut from me the behavior that aggravated him. I forgave. I started again. But the violence continued. Eventually I began to feel that, no matter how I changed — even if I became the perfect woman — he would still be able to find an excuse for his abuse.

I went through a period of immense confusion. We had times of great happiness interspersed with intervals of bitter criticism of every aspect of my behavior. We had periods when the harmony that seemed to come turned out to be a veneer to hide relationships with other women. We experienced many moments when an unconsidered comment instantly tipped the scales from tranquillity to an explosiveness that stunned us both. I reached the stage where I doubted my self-worth, I doubted my sexuality, I doubted my wisdom.

But one day — a day when I felt I had touched the depths of desperation — a miracle happened. I went outside to look in the letter-box — just for the sake of doing something really in an effort to drag myself up a little. I was not expecting any mail. There I found the Word of Life of the month. I remember that I nearly didn't bother to open it. I was almost on the point of throwing it in the bin. But something stopped me. I opened it and read it.

Those words shone out at me with a light and a truth, that took my breath away. They became imprinted on my soul and in my very being. From that moment right up to today in every suffering and in every joy they have remained with me with the same impact they had then.

"We know that everything works for the good of those who love God."

The moment I read those words I understood for the first time that the only thing I had to do was love God. I understood that if I wanted to love him he would show me how. I knew all of a sudden and with great certainty that God would be able to draw good from the desperate situation I found myself in. I had the certainty that this good would emerge even if I was unaware of it or unable to grasp it. I experienced the immensity of God's love through these words: as though he had said them for me, as though they had just been uttered for the first time in all eternity, as though he wanted to reach me in my suffering, sustain me and embrace me to the point of filling me to overflowing with his love.

And so once more I began again. But this time it was different: it was no longer out of habit or pride or because I thought it was the right thing to do. It was out of love for God.

I tried to set aside my ideas to love only him. I kept repeating over and over to myself: "We know that everything works for the good of those who love God." My part was easy—all I had to do was love him! And as I tried to be faithful to this resolution I began to understand how I had to change.

Perhaps it was this change in me which touched Bob, I don't know, but five months later he agreed to attend a five-day meeting of the Focolare movement together with me. The decision to go together was a miracle in itself, as, for many years, Bob had been dubious about the Focolare and its ideals.

As an outward success for me, that meeting was a dismal failure, but inwardly our miracle started. One act of violence there among all that love showed the way in which I had to love Bob. I finally realized that it wasn't love to hold him in a situation where he wasn't able to change. I understood that it was pride to think that it was my love that would eventually first touch him. Like a revelation, I saw that I had to let go of my life and hand control over to God. I guess that, until then, I thought my judgment to be better than His! With that letting go came the grace to give an ultimatum—"If there's any more violence, I'll leave you."

In the weeks that followed we tried, almost with brute force, to break away from the past. The tension became unbearable so we decided that we — or rather I — would benefit from a brief period of rest with the children.

But there were times when the suffering tore me apart. I was pregnant and drained and I eventually ended up in a hospital far from home. I wondered whether I was really doing God's will. Did I have the right to face a suffering if it could affect our unborn baby? I didn't seem to have enough strength to banish the doubts, let alone love Jesus crucified and forsaken.

The light of the Word of Life which had helped me so much seemed to be extinguished and at times I felt I was stupid to cling to it. But cling to it I did with an obstinate faith in God's love: "We know that everything works for the good of those who love God."

I returned home but a short time later the violence erupted again. So it was that I packed my bags and left him. With God's grace I was able to accept his demands that our two beautiful children should remain with him. I knew that, finally, I was really loving him. And I knew that, in stepping off my cliff in faith, I was giving God a chance to carry me to the fulfillment of his plans — whatever they were.

After the baby was born, we decided to have one final attempt at starting again. Before I came home — and many times afterwards — I doubted the wisdom of that decision. Surely life would be so much calmer if I lived by myself. I could do what I wanted when I wanted. I wouldn't have to bother with the effort of trying to support — or even just exist with — Bob while he was going through this traumatic period of counselling. I wouldn't have to change myself — no cutting or pruning; what a wonderful temptation when you're tired and drained! Surely the price of emptiness was a small one to pay for this. I didn't even really believe that we would ever be capable of sharing the joys of married love.

I know how much God loves me, because he niggled and pushed and prodded inside me until I was able to cut from all of these temptations and doubts. I re-read those words with all my soul: "We know that everything works for the good of those who love God," and took another giant leap off my cliff of doubts. I can still remember how stupid I thought I was to be stepping back into a situation that had brought about so much suffering. The miracle was that I understood that all I had to do was give my hundred percent—if that was only a fraction of what was needed, then God would happily do the rest.

So I came home. The greatest gift to us over that time was the knowledge that so many people had us in their hearts and prayers. This was a period of such cutting and changing that I would never have thought possible. Sometimes I complained: "Surely there must be an easier way to love you Lord!" But he continued to show the way and always gave us the grace we needed.

I finally really understood that changing isn't a matter of taking off one coat and putting on another. I saw Bob pouring all his strength into pulling himself apart and gouging out all those ways opposed to love that had roots deep down inside him. With his example and support I worked—and am still working—at bringing down my defenses, at opening my heart, at trusting. But these barriers to love aren't just walls around me. After all these years of hurt, they are part of me. Every day when I try to say yes to God and to love with all my heart, I'm really offering to "cut off my hand and gouge out my eye." It's not an easy decision, but that just makes it a more beautiful gift that I can give to him—and to give to someone you love is always a great joy.

The struggle inside me to learn anew to trust seemed neverending. But I continued to seek and to pray that God would show me the way to open my heart and make it vulnerable.

Some time passed and I learned I had a brain tumor. An urgent operation had to be performed. In the hospital following the operation, despite the incredible love and harmony that had gradually grown between us, I found I was afraid to return home. I realized for the first time in my life that I had nothing: no physical resources, nothing to lean on if things went wrong, no way of helping Bob who was tired and worn-out from looking after the family during my stay in hospital. I was truly empty. I had nothing. I had to go home and I was afraid. "We know that everything works for the good of those who love God"—*my* Word of Life. Again it was there to give me strength. And in my heart a renewed offering to God: "If you want it Lord, I want it, too. Empty-handed, but with peace in my heart I will go home." The hundredfold came and filled my heart. All my defenses and barriers crumbled and were swept away leaving room for a new flowering of love between Bob and me that I would never have dreamed possible. And in my heart there remains the absolute conviction that "everything works for the good of those who love God."

*Bob:* I grew up in an atmosphere of violence and anger. My parents often argued and threatened each other. Many nights were spent as a child crying myself to sleep out of fear and the frustration that no matter how I tried the arguments continued.

As I got older the atmosphere seemed to change at home; life appeared to be settling down with fewer outbursts of violence. However, this was not really the case at all. I was building a wall around myself to protect myself from the feelings that this atmosphere created in me. I trusted only in myself, not in my parents and certainly not anyone else. The wall I had built to protect myself had become a barrier through which I could not reach or be reached.

All throughout my schooling at a church school I was hearing about God and yet living a life of misery and suffering. Not being capable of trusting, I discovered that I doubted that God could really exist, otherwise there would not be all this suffering in my family.

By the time I finished school there was already a lot of anger and resentment locked inside me. My parents found a job for me without consulting me about it. I was shocked and very angry that my parents did not feel that I could find a job for myself or a least talk it over with me.

So I started work with a lot of resentment. At the time I was unaware of this feeling, but it certainly had a great effect on me and my relationship with the people I worked with, who endured a very angry and touchy co-worker.

When I was in my early twenties I met Mary, a person unlike anyone I had ever met and who seemed to be genuinely interested in me. One day she invited me to Mass with her. This was the first time I had ever attended Mass, and eventually I started to attend with her more or less regularly, though at that time I did not understand why.

As Mary and I spent more time together we became very attached to each other. In Mary's case a love for me developed, and in my own case I felt that here was someone I could trust and be myself with, though at that time I really believed it was love. Before we married, an incident occurred that was to shape our future and cause a great deal of suffering and pain for both of us, and in later years, for those people, family and friends, who love us. Mary and I were driving somewhere or other when we started to argue and at the peak of the argument I slapped her, totally without thinking. This came as a shock to Mary who had never encountered anything like it in her life. I was angry with Mary for having got me so mad that this should happen — it wasn't difficult to justify my actions to myself at this time.

No matter how I look at it now, this was physical violence being expressed by me toward Mary, though at the time I felt that it was Mary who was wrong and not myself and that in fact it was her provocation that caused this violence to manifest itself. Never for one moment did I stop to think that the problem we were facing, or as I understand it now, that Mary was facing, was within me and not Mary. Over the next few years the violence became more pronounced, the excuses more frequent and the justification much stronger. I felt the problem was not mine but caused from outside, by Mary. After nearly eleven years of marriage with Mary making excuses for my behavior as well as her own, our relationship was really suffering, for Mary if not for me. Though I felt very guilty and remorseful, after each act of violence, I always felt the justification that I had been pushed past my limit before I retaliated.

Finally, about eight years ago, Mary felt she had to separate to protect herself and the children from a very evil situation. And so Mary and the children left to go and stay with Mary's family for an extended "holiday" so that there would be time to review the situation. As time went by I felt more convinced that Mary was imagining problems and that they were not as bad as was being made out. During this time Mary became very ill and was put into hospital, being five months pregnant at the time. This for the first time in my life made me become concerned for someone other than myself. While Mary was in the hospital, her brother, Mike, came and saw me to let me know that he would give any help or support that I needed. I thought that this was only because he was trying to help Mary and because he was a very religious man, but other people I knew from the Focolare movement offered the same support. After a month Mary and the children came back home and, for two weeks, everything seemed fine. However a situation eventually arose where I became violent again. Mary felt that she could not go on trying in the same way, to put love into our situation, especially as every assurance I gave was very soon broken.

For the second time Mary was forced to leave home, but this time I managed (manipulated) to get her to leave the children with me on the excuse that her health still was not up to looking after them. As long as I controlled the children I felt that I controlled our situation and that given time she would see the error of her ways.

A couple of days went by with me starting to realize that wives don't just sit at home all day and do what suits them, when Mary's brother rang me and asked if I would like him to come and stay with me for company. I said that it would really be wonderful if he could as I was feeling very lonely and isolated. He would listen as I poured out all my anger and frustrations. Night after night we would sit while I vented my feelings, yet throughout all of this he had a peace about him that I started to notice. He only looked at the positive never the negative aspects of each situation. During this period with Mike I slowly began to realize that all the anger I was directing at Mary might just be because there was something wrong inside myself. One night while we were preparing dinner I asked Mike if he thought it might be a good idea to get some professional help to sort out the turmoil in my mind. He thought this was a positive step in the right direction and that if I really worked at discovering the real causes of my violent behavior Mary would in time come back and be prepared to give our marriage another try.

Throughout Mike's stay with me he was a shining example of what love is through his constant love for me and Mary, even to the point of forgetting his own suffering. It was during these days that I understood what is meant by "Where there is no love put love and love will grow." For the first time I believed that someone loved me, and what had been a friendship with Mike started to grow into a love that continues to grow as I was learning how to live in charity. This then was a start. I quickly came to realize that I didn't know how to love and that this among other things had been the cause of my behavior. I believe in my heart that the Word of Life was bringing about a dramatic turn around in my life and that the ugly part of me was slowly being shed.

One day, I remember thinking that all the gifts of love that Mary had over the years given or done for me were gone forever and I felt an anguish that was more painful than anything I had ever known. The pain grew for a time until through prayer I knew that I had to look forward and let go of the past. Some time later when reflecting on our life together I discovered that these gifts of Mary's were there in front of me unopened. We had together shared these most beautiful gifts and they were now all the more beautiful since my love for Mary is growing stronger with every experience we live through and share.

Mary and I were able through the prayers and support of our friends around us to start a new life together, a life that, for me did not consist of thinking only of myself and no one else.

Recently Mary and I lived through our greatest experience together. Mary underwent surgery for the removal of a tumor in the base of her brain. Whereas, a year ago or so, I would have become angry at this affliction on our life, I was able to see how through this suffering we were growing in love and unity. We were being given a gift so precious and great if only we could embrace it, something I knew Mary could do because of her faith, but which I feared that I might not be able to cope with. Early in the morning I went to Mass feeling ill at ease because I was finding it difficult to pray for Mary. During the Mass I felt closer to Jesus than at any other time in my life. I then noticed that my fear was not as great and I could pray.

I left Mass with a feeling of peace so great that I knew I was not alone. Jesus was with me as I lived this day. During the day while the operation was under way I had a glimpse of the love God has for us, and I realized that through these experiences my faith has grown alongside my capacity to love.

*M. and B. R.*

## 11.
## What Profit is There . . . ?

*"What profit would a man show if he were to gain the whole world and destroy himself in the process?"* (Mt 16:26).

Let's take careful note of these words of Jesus. His reasoning surpasses a prudence of a human level that might suggest: what does it serve to accumulate riches if later on we are only going to die anyway?

What Jesus is saying has much greater depth than this. In order to understand it, let's see what he means by the word "soul." This term does not refer to the spiritual soul, which is distinct from the body; it means a number of things: life, being, the whole person. In other words, "to lose one's soul" can mean: to find blocked the way to eternal life. If a person loses one's soul, nothing can make one happy, not even possession of the entire world. In fact, there is no price high enough to ransom back the soul.

*"What profit would a man show if he were to gain the whole world and destroy himself in the process?"*

Material gain is a very common component in the life of society. Often, however, when limits are exceeded, the human person can become completely absorbed by it. This is where the mistake lies.

The most important thing is the very being of the human person, the whole person, who is called to live in communion with God already here on earth and then eternally in the next life.

"Having" is not so important. Therefore, if one muddles about from morning to evening in things that are only secondary, values become inverted; what is necessary and fundamental loses its place.

*"What profit would a man show if he were to gain the whole world and destroy himself in the process?"*

By saying this, Jesus is not teaching us to despise the world, for it is itself a work of God. Just the same, he is putting us on our guard not to make earthly goods the whole of our existence, but rather to use them in such a way as to not allow them to take the place of God in our hearts.

Jesus opens our eyes to the true dimensions of this short life of ours. Our life is a journey, on course toward a splendid goal. It would be a great mistake to confine it, or restrict it to the things of this earth. One day we will lose our life, because its time will run out, and along with it we will lose the next life. If we foolishly attach ourselves to things that pass away, that other life will not be there for us.

Therefore, we must journey in time, but with our hearts linked to the eternal.

*"What profit would a man show if he were to gain the whole world and destroy himself in the process?"*

To come to a better understanding of how we can live this word of Jesus, let's look to the truly wise, the saints. They did not hoard up goods for themselves: they gave them to the poor. Thus, they lived in authentic freedom, so as to adhere to the only good that guarantees true life, Christ. In fact, it is he who is life. The complete fulfillment of every human person can be found in him.

Let's allow ourselves to say no to the disordinate aspirations which arise from our egos. Are we disposed to put aside everything that can obstruct the presence of God in our lives? Let's ask ourselves each evening whether he has always been in the first place. If it is so, we will have gained, along with joy, peace, and love, which are fruits of the kingdom within us, also increased light and strength in order to make our contribution toward building a new world already here below.

*Chiara Lubich*

## *Out to get that money?*

Mine is an experience of trying to live as a peacemaker, someone who tries to generate mutual understanding, in my case, in the business world of New York City. Within and between companies there are war games. Possibly some of the greatest war-making in the world goes on there.

I work for a multi-billion dollar company in the communications industry. It is one of the most competitive fields there is. I work in the magazine division and I am a sales manager. We try to get advertising for our magazine.

I have had to ask myself what my attitude is towards our competitors, and towards the people whom I service.

Recently our business was down drastically by almost seven million dollars. My boss told me to get some of it back. Now, I have learned that you have to project a certain aggressiveness which demonstrates that you are "out to get that money," but in reality, I was doing it to make him happy. I feel that there is nothing wrong with making my boss successful. We have a good product and we offer a good service. I feel I can be in unity with him in this. But it doesn't mean that I have to go out and exploit my clients just to make my boss happy because I have to love my clients as well.

In this case, however, in order to accomplish my goal, I searched for a good reason why my client should advertise in our magazine. I targeted a particular account where I thought that it would do some good and I demonstrated how if they did advertise with us it would showcase a new product that they were coming out with. I obtained some very good positioning for them in the magazine and so forth. They were very, very pleased and gave us the account. It also happens that I have a very good personal relationship with this client. It is a relationship that has been built up over the years and we are truly friends.

We were all happy . . . but what about the competitor? We live in a very imperfect world. In order to give us the business, the client had to turn down another magazine. How can you handle cases like this? How do you deal with those people of other magazines who also need an income? I don't have a real clear answer to that but I'll just share the attitude that I try to maintain.

Our competitors also take business from me from one month to the next and it has become like a volleyball game between good friends. I play very hard for my team but my attitude is that when the other team wins I am happy for them. This, in fact, is really the effort I am making.

Hopefully things will change in the system in the future but for now I cannot exit from this imperfect world. I try to care for those competitors and be happy when they do take business from me. But it also means taking risks.

For example, we have many industry-wide events where competitors are all together. There is a lot of tension in these events because we all know we are pretty much at each other's throats.

New or young people who come to these events very often don't really know what's going on, or who the big clients are. Many times I give them the names of the people they should call on. In a sense, you could say that I am cutting my own throat.

In another case, I once recommended a very good sales person to a competitive magazine and now he's selling against me. I did this in order to help him get a job and he succeeded in getting it with my recommendation.

My experience is, however, that when you maintain this attitude, things do work out. You would think that I'd be losing business but actually I have been very successful. Three years ago the entire company was re-organized and a very tough management team came in and literally swept everyone away. We were seventeen sales people and after the change-over I was the only one left. I really think it was because of this attitude. I find that as I go around, making my contacts, people, even on the side of the competition, are saying nice things about me.

My task as I see it is to continue as a peacemaker in this competitive environment as we try, with wisdom, to work toward a more perfect system.

*S. L.*

## *Success at any cost*

God has always had his hand on my head. When I was born I was a still-birth. After trying, unsuccessfully, to bring me around the doctor laid me aside as dead. The next-door neighbor who had assisted the doctor decided to try to revive me — what could she lose — I was dead anyway. She was successful. I guess God had his plans for me.

I did not have an ordinary child's life. In fact, I sometimes wonder if I had a childhood. By the time I was ten my parents were divorced. My mother had to go to work, to keep the little family together, so I became the little mother at home. We lived in abject poverty.

I did not like to be poor. I developed a consciousness of unworthiness in my personality. I continually dreamt of a better life. In fact, I dreamt of a "Shangri-la."

Poor children find some way of entertaining themselves, and mine was reading. I found that I could read in the library without any cost, so I spent many, many hours there. My mother couldn't afford the kind of education I wanted. Books were at my disposal, so I would get my education that way. I knew I must have an education if I wanted to complete my dream. And this dream was never to be poor again. I felt the rich had everything!

The years passed. I married. I was busy with the children but my dream still persisted. Someday I would have that better life.

After the children grew up I got a job I liked. I learned everything I could about it and started my own business.

Seeing other people in business, I felt that you could not have friends in business. So I plunged myself into work, and as far as people were concerned, I would use them to further my cause. My favorite saying was, "God helps those that help themselves." I was going to be successful at any cost. I felt if people were not successful, it was their own fault, because they hadn't tried.

Before I had the business, my marriage was not going so well, so now that I had the business, I plunged myself into it and used it as a haven to escape from home. If I came home before my husband was asleep, there was quarrelling. I began to feel that I had no home. As long as I had work at the studio it was bearable, but many times there wasn't enough work in the evening to keep me busy. Sometimes I would walk in the downtown section trying to find some distraction for my tortured mind. I truly felt I was alone in the world. Of course, I consoled myself that the higher you went in any endeavor the more alone your life would be because you left the people who could understand your level of life. On each higher level, there were fewer people of your kind. I pictured the most successful person on earth completely alone, because there was no one in his class. He had something that no one else had, but he had to pay a price, of course, of loneliness. Everything had a price. You got nothing for free. A successful person had no need of people. If they couldn't communicate with him on his level they were to be discarded. These were some of the things I learned through the success books I devoured whenever I could. I always felt one must pay for success — and I was willing to do it. If you weren't willing to pay, then, you didn't deserve it.

Somehow, the price was pretty steep for what you got — for example, tense nerves, which tie up the whole system. If you lived this way for a prolonged period of time your body began to break down. I saw many business people collapse over their desks and wheeled out to the ambulance. Many never came back.

In my case I was also nervous, short-tempered, and had a disgust for people who were slow thinkers. Slowly and insidiously I was sinking into a mire which was enveloping my life. I was suffocating. I was not free. I was not happy. I had to make more money, more quickly, so that I could afford a life of ease and freedom.

In the meantime this bucket of worms was eating away my very life. I was fearful that the sand of time would pour out before I could reach my goal. I had to work harder, watch competition, not trust anyone — they were all out to put me out of business if I was not vigilant.

I also had a need for competent employees. The work was exacting and people have long stopped being craftsmen. Everyone wanted a job where they could file their nails while they got paid — with coffee breaks yet. I was desperate. I advertised, again, in the newspaper.

One girl came. I interviewed her but I didn't think she had

what I needed. "I'll hire her," I told myself, "and when other applicants, who are more efficient, come, I'll get rid of her."

She came from Brazil, had a heavy accent, and had some difficulty with the language. I needed a sharp girl who had a command of the English language, who could spell, type fairly fast, knew her punctuation, knew composition, layout and paste-up. She was exactly the opposite. She had a desperate need for a job and had a beautiful defense when asked if she knew how to do anything. She always answered, "You will see."

Somehow she managed from day to day. In the meantime no one else showed up for the job. She had a sweet disposition. I attributed that to the fact that the Latin people were warm-hearted. She worked hard, and I didn't have to get after her to keep busy. This girl was different — what was it? Are there some people in the world who aren't out to get everything they can for the mighty dollar? She began to grow on me, in spite of the fact that I felt the way I did.

She had friends who came in at noon. They all went to lunch together. She would get back on time and get to work. She always seemed to have extra lunch at her table and she munched while she worked. After she was with me about a week she asked for a favor. "Okay, what is the favor?" She needed more time for lunch — she wanted to add her rest period to her lunch time. Suspicion gripped me — here it starts — first this, then what next? I didn't like changes! Nevertheless, I allowed it. Her friends joined her in thanking me.

What was so important that would cause this much joy? I had to know why she needed this extra time. I inquired and she told me that she used her lunch time to go to Mass and could barely get her lunch from the restaurant in time to bring it to her table, to munch on later.

Slowly I was taken by this tiny bit of humanity and her beautiful friends. I plied her with questions. She was not anxious to answer, but I was persistent. I wanted to know more about her. On the application she put Brazil as her birthplace. So I questioned her about her family and about Brazil. Her family was in politics in Brazil. She said she had just arrived in Chicago from New York. Before that she had been in school in Italy. I wondered why she would want to work here, in Chicago, if her people were so prominent in Brazil. Looking at her I surmised she could be no more than eighteen or nineteen years of age, but she seemed to have traveled a lot and was educated abroad. So again, I plied her with questions. She said she had a rich father. I didn't reckon with "her idea" of a rich father. So I was satisfied with the idea of a rich man's daughter wanting to travel and have her own experiences—why not?

When her friends came there was such joy and the same interest bubbled among them. From wisps of conversation I caught things that interested me. I am insatiably curious, so back to the questions. Why would such different girls have a common interest. One was Italian, one Brazilian and the other American, yet they had a common bond. They said that they wanted to start a Christian revolution. I was looking for a revolution, even though I didn't know it.

Deep down I was looking for a better life. It really was fair game.

Before long I was going to Mass along with them. We constantly talked about Jesus. I could hardly believe that so much beauty existed within the reach of anyone who wanted it. Slowly suspicion turned to trust. I wanted to be with them all the time. When I was alone I would be in danger of falling back into my old ways.

No matter what mistakes I would make, through charity, I was not exposed to ridicule. I was loved despite all my faults. Their love burned away the imperfections. Little by little I began to love too. I learned to accept myself along with all the other people. It was an amazement to me that I could love everyone. When I began to see with the eyes of love, there were nothing but beautiful people who were misled by their "love-starved" thoughts.

Revolution is a mild word to express what took place in my soul! My life took on a new meaning. The God I thought I believed in—who was somewhere in a far-off land—became a personal God. I found myself conversing with a living God. I found myself so full of love that at times I don't think my feet touched the ground as I walked. I was alive. I was free. God made the world and gave me dominion over it—the whole world was mine. What else did I need? God was good. He loved me and I loved Him. Now I live in love. And I also have a "Rich Father."

*R. K.*

# 12.
# The Rights of God and Those of Caesar

*"Then give to Caesar what is Caesar's, but give to God what is God's"* (Mt 22:21).

This sentence, in its simplicity, is a very rich and enlightening one for all of us, for each of us lives on a given point of the earth, is an expression of a particular people, and each one is part of a specific nation.

But on what occasion did Jesus speak these words?

The Jews were forced into paying the Romans a tax, which was the humiliating sign of their submission to a foreign power, and at that, a pagan one. Such a fact constituted an intolerable scandal for a people who recognized Yahweh as their only sovereign. Such a situation offered an occasion for the Pharisees—who were not the least enthused about Jesus' popularity—to set a trap for him, so they sent some of their disciples along with a group of Herodians to pose him a question: "Is it lawful to pay tax to the emperor or not?" The question did constitute a real trap because, had Jesus answered yes, the Herodians being of the Roman line and the Pharisees of a wider, more independent current, the Pharisees would have had the chance to accuse him before the people as a sympathizer to the Romans, as one who has been bribed, and therefore would have set against him the entire anti-Roman current; but if, on the contrary, he had answered no, the Herodians would have been able to denounce him as an enemy of the Romans, an instigator, an extremist.

Jesus on this occasion asks them to show him the silver coin with which to pay the tax and to tell him whose image and inscription is stamped on the coin. They responded by saying it is that of Caesar. Jesus then retorted, "Then give to Caesar what is Caesar's, but give to God what is God's." Practically speaking, Jesus is telling them: "If the coin has any use to you, it must mean that gladly or not, you recognize Caesar's authority; therefore, you should pay the tax."

So Jesus is not against paying taxes to the authority: moreover, he implicitly admits that it must be done. The important thing for him does not lie so much in the fact of having to pay the tax to the Roman emperor, but rather in giving one's heart and soul to God.

*"Then give to Caesar what is Caesar's, but give to God what is God's."*

Different interpretations have been given to this particular phrase. In any case, what seems clear is the great freedom that Jesus shows in regard to political power. He appears as a man who is truly free in the face of the Herodians, who have yielded to the power of Rome and to a totalitarian ideology that goes so far as to divinize the emperor. Equally so, he is also free before the Pharisees, slaves of a theocratic mentality, whose cause for God rests on the political liberation of the country. Extending the invitation to love God above all things, Jesus takes away any kind of support for the totalitarian state to which the Herodians gave their allegiance, and to the theocratic state sought after by the Pharisees. At the same time he indirectly places his disciples — whether they hold important positions or are simply ordinary citizens — in the ideal condition to fulfill their civil duties in a spirit of service to their fellow human beings who make up the political community.

*"Then give to Caesar what is Caesar's, but give to God what is God's."*

How can we live this Word of Life? It urges us, even though indirectly, to make or to renew and to live the choice of God and the preeminence of his love in our social and political responsibilities and in the fulfillment of our duties toward the state. It helps us, first of all, to avoid two equally grave and opposite dangers. One consists in a mistrust and disinterest in political involvement, as though it were something evil, a field of activity reserved only for malicious people. The other consists in an exaggerated trust that lends itself to an excessive haste in looking for the results that political involvement can bring. The gospel must certainly penetrate political and social activities, but this will only be possible in the measure in which those called to work in such areas are sure to place God above all else and translate this love into true service of the society, in a spirit of detachment, patience and perseverance.

More concretely speaking, those who are called to work actively in this field must make of their activity a true service to the human person, giving first preference to the poor and to the least. What comes to mind here are all the occasions in which, not only public officials and congressmen, but all government employees from the highest to the more modest positions, must live their choice of God through the most selfless, punctual, and dedicated service to all. One such occasion can be a more speedy and diligent response to every individual's rightful requests or a more efficient handling of documents that are of service to them.

*"Then give to Caesar what is Caesar's, but give to God what is God's."*

In regard to being ordinary citizens, this Word of Life urges all to carry out faithfully their duties toward the state and to reach an ever greater sense of responsibility toward the common good. It is a Christian duty, for example, to cast their vote in the political and administrative elections, unless they are inhibited to do so by circumstances beyond their control. Avoiding evasions and the like, it is a duty to pay one's taxes, without which the state cannot assure the services the community needs. It is likewise important to contribute, according to allowable means, to the betterment of the general public. It is a Christian duty to respect the law, which serves to safeguard the life and good of its citizens, as it is also a duty to feel responsible for the conservation of the goods of the collectivity: public buildings, streets, gardens, forests, landscapes, means of transportation, and so on. In all these instances, the following words of Jesus can be applied: "I assure you, as often as you did it for one of my least brothers, you did it for me" (Mt 25:40). Ultimately, the services we perform are rendered for Jesus himself, who is loved in the concrete person of our neighbor.

We must be grateful to have such varied and frequent opportunities to do so.

*Chiara Lubich*

## *A manager in Dallas*

I am a manager in the hotel business in Dallas. Because of the service nature of the business and rigorous time frames, the turnover of employees and the stress in general is very high. Consequently, the supervisors are often very young and unseasoned when dealing especially with personnel problems.

Recently an employee committed a very serious violation of company policy which required immediate action on the part of management. When I was informed of the violation, I knew it not only called for swift action, but needed to be handled delicately and with discretion. If the situation were not handled properly, it could have a very negative effect on this employee's reputation and even on his ability to find work in the future. It also had the potential of placing the company in an unfavorable legal position.

My first reaction was to "take the bull by the horns" and handle the problem swiftly and properly. I knew though, that the right thing to do was to go through the proper chain of command and let the employee's immediate supervisor take care of the matter. I also knew that this supervisor was a young man who had no previous experience in a matter so sensitive. I had to step in and take control; that was my job. However, just stepping in and handling it by myself would not be love for my neighbor, and I kept remembering that the greatest commandment of all is to love one's neighbor as oneself. If I just handled it myself, he would not grow in his career, nor would he know that I trust his ability as a manager.

I decided to invite Sam, the supervisor, to my office, and I really tried to place myself in his shoes. I told him of the problem, and how the situation was extremely delicate. I asked him for his help. "It is just too big for either of us to handle alone," I explained. Sam indicated his agreement. I went on to say that even though this employee had really hurt us, the company, first we had to be sensitive to him, and only then, we had to consider the action we must take. So without having quoted chapter and verse, I felt he had understood that we had to love our neighbor.

Together we called the employee into the office. In management training we are taught ways to take control of a situation so that the person being reprimanded feels intimidated and is more likely to react in a "positive" manner. I thought about this beforehand. We could bring the employee into my office and seat him in front of my big oak desk and have him in the palm of our hands. I knew though that this would not be living the gospel and I remembered a phrase from scripture, "We must make ourselves all things to all men."

When the employee arrived, I took all of us to a seating area with easy chairs and a small table between us. Everyone was more relaxed. As the conversation started a look of deep anxiety appeared on the face of the employee. But as our talk went on, I could see him becoming more at ease even though it was evident that his job would be terminated. The facts and points of concern were discussed rather than fingers being pointed. When we ended, he stood up, we all shook hands, and I wished him luck in the future.

When I turned to look at Sam, his face was puzzled. It was as though he couldn't believe that instead of using an ax on the employee, we had used paper scissors. But he realized that the same results had been accomplished. I asked Sam how he thought it went. After a long and thoughtful hesitation, he said: "That was nice. That was really nice." He turned and walked out the door.

Near the end of the day, I was at my desk, concentrating on a letter that I had just received. When I looked up, Sam was standing directly in front of the desk, staring at me. Not knowing how long he had been standing there, I said, "I didn't see you standing there." Sam said, "I didn't want to go home tonight without telling you that what you did today was really nice." There was such genuineness in his voice that I experienced joy in hearing his words again. Then I said, "It's not what I did today, Sam. It's what we did together." With a big grin, he nodded and left the office.

*D. M.*

## *A new rapport*

I am in the U.S. Air Force. Recently, I was promoted to the rank of sergeant which means I became a supervisor for several people. As supervisor, I am responsible for each person's well-being both on as well as off duty.

When I was first assigned this new responsibility, I decided the first thing I could do was work at building a stronger unity between my supervisors and myself. I talked openly with all of them to find out what they expected from me. Right away we established a new rapport which seemed to enable us to talk things out.

In turn, each was glad to give back his support. Most also gave valuable advice and encouraged me to ask for help whenever I needed it.

Then the test arrived. One of the individuals whom I supervise had been in the service only a couple of months. He had gotten into serious trouble and I learned that the commanders were seeking possible judicial action. I knew it was my responsibility to try to love in the midst of regulations, and therefore investigate the case, rather than just let the matter take its course.

First, I decided to get to know this individual better. I checked his records and saw that he had been doing excellent work on duty. We had several discussions in private and I learned that he was a good person who was, however, having some problems adjusting. It seemed clear that his mistake was an aberration, atypical of past behavior.

My responsibility, therefore, was to explain to the commanders this other side of the individual which I had seen.

To do this, though, took a lot of courage. All of my supervisors are older, more experienced and have much more rank than I have. I realized that I had to trust in God in order to have that forcefulness which would result in the commanders reviewing the case. Each time that I went in, it was an either or situation: Die to myself and work on this case, or let the situation continue on the path that was standard procedure. I kept opting for what I thought would be building unity.

The final outcome was good. The commanders weighted heavily our judgment and lowered the punishment from possible loss of rank, wages and confinement to a letter of reprimand which can be taken away in the future with good conduct.

Later the head supervisor thanked me. He said, "The only reason it turned out the way it did was because you cared."

The "hundredfold" though came when he said that he too had learned a lesson. He saw a need to establish a new rapport with all the workers in order to increase unity in our area.

*D. L.*

## *Jury duty*

My wife and I were very involved in planning a meeting we had been looking forward to for a long time. The week prior to this meeting, which was to be held in the place where I worked, I was selected for jury duty.

Part of my responsibility for the meeting was to have keys to certain rooms and areas and to be present to see that all the facilities were open and available.

I had never served as a juror before so this was a totally new experience for me. The case was a murder trial and it was a difficult case in that conflicting evidence and testimony were presented. The jurors were an interesting group of persons. We had never seen one another before but during the time we were together we got well acquainted. The group was very mixed in every way. We had men and women; Blacks, Hispanics, Anglos. We had many occupations represented—a teacher, a railroad engineer, an office manager, a minister's wife, a university professor and others. We ranged widely in age with the youngest being a young woman, a recent college graduate who had majored in criminal justice.

As the days went on we became somewhat more tense as the severity of the crime was evident—a man had been killed—but we had to decide if the alleged murderer was in fact the man who committed the crime or not, and if we found him guilty we had to come up with the sentence.

We occasionally had an informal vote to see if we were in agreement. Because everything was not crystal clear, many of us saw things differently from time to time. When we had been together for a week, and many were becoming tense from being away from their jobs, and maybe losing pay of business, there was a heightened tenseness among the group.

I was preoccupied with our meeting when by Friday we were still not in agreement as a jury and the meeting was to begin the very next day. I left the house that morning giving my keys to my wife, saying, "I may not be with you for the meeting as the judge could sequester us for the weekend and not let us return to our homes if we don't reach a unanimous verdict."

One of the nice things about jury duty is that you are taken as a group each noon for lunch. Prior to going to lunch that Friday, our group was at a point where eleven of us were of one opinion about the verdict, but the young woman who had majored in criminal justice had an opposite opinion. Some of the group of jurors, because of their tenseness and exhaustion with the whole experience, began to badger her and were somewhat less than kind. The more they tried to persuade her the more stubborn she became to where it seemed a battle of the wills. We were taken to a hotel restaurant that day by the bailiff and by chance I found myself sitting next to this young lady. During the week she had told us of her father's birthday and how her family celebrated it and what gift she gave her father. I knew that my responsibility was to love this young woman in a Christian way, emptying myself of my concerns and preoccupations and concentrating on her — doing in my own way what Jesus did for us, that is, lay down my life, in this case my preoccupations and my will, to do the will of God for me.

I talked and listened to the young woman about her family, about her father and his birthday party, about the gift, which was a cordless telephone, about which I knew little, and we talked about how it worked and how much her father would enjoy that gift. We made no mention of the trial, of our fellow jurors.

As we were being driven back to the court and the jury room which by now seemed like a prison for us, the young woman said to the rest of the group, "We may have a unanimous decision soon." Once we were in the jury room by ourselves as a group of twelve, she explained to the others that they had not treated her with respect, that they had badgered her and that they made her angry and resistant. On the contrary, she went on to say, "this man" (meaning me) has treated me kindly, has not tried to pressure me, and I feel free to state my position about this case.

Within a matter of a few hours the trial was over, I was on my way home and the next day was present for the beautiful gathering I was hoping to attend.

*B. G.*